WAKE UP
LISTEN
UP

OR

GO DOWN

WAKE UP
LISTEN
UP
OR
GO DOWN

ROBERT "BOB"
DOBRANSKI, MDiv

ARPress
ILLUMINATING IDEAS
EMPOWERING VOICES

ARPress
45 Dan Road Suite 5
Canton MA 02021

Hotline: 1(888) 821-0229
Fax: 1(508) 545-7580

Ordering Information:
Quantity sales. Special discounts are available on quantity purchases by corporations, associations, and others. For details, contact the publisher at the address above.

Printed in the United States of America.

ISBN-13:   Paperback   979-8-89389-666-4
              eBook   979-8-89389-667-1

Library of Congress Control Number: 2024923863

TABLE OF CONTENTS

DEDICATION

Blessed is he who reads and those who hear the words of the prophecy, and heed the things which are written in it; for the time is near (Revelation 1:3).

ALL SCRIPTURE REFERENCES ARE FROM
THE NEW AMERICAN STANDARD BIBLE (NASB)
UNLESS OTHERWISE INDICATED.

Robert "Bob" Dobranski.
TWTG_Promo@Yahoo.com

ACKNOWLEDGMENTS

To all teachers who positively influenced their students but were never thanked for a job well done!

INTRODUCTION

This book is about the ministry of the Two Prophets in The Book of the Revelation, but it will also be a challenge to the people of The Way to see if their lives and ministries are aligned with the Prophets Teachings and Ministry. If they are aligned you are blessed in the Lord. However, if they are not aligned, you must Wake Up, Listen Up, or Go Down.

> *"But you, brethren, are not in darkness, that the day should overtake you like a thief; for you are all sons of light and sons of day. 'We are not of night nor of darkness; so then let us not sleep as others do, but let us be alert and sober'" (1 Thessalonians 5:4-6).*

Many have attempted to write about and even make movies about the Two Witnesses in The Book of Revelation. However, all those works focus on what the Two Witnesses will **do** rather than focusing on what **they will say.** What they do is only a sidebar issue to their Verbal Testimony. The things that they do will be God's confirming signs that what they are witnessing too is "the only true Gospel." They are the

Lord's Witnesses "My *two witnesses*" "*And I will grant authority to My two witnesses*" (Revelation. 11:3).

The judgments that follow the teachings of the Two Witnesses are like when God raised His Son from the dead. The Son's Resurrection from the dead was God's "declaration" that His Son's sacrificial work on the cross was efficacious enough to take away our sins; and not for ours only, but also for those of the whole world.

> *Paul, a bond-servant of Christ Jesus, called as an apostle, set apart for the gospel of God, which He promised beforehand through His prophets in the holy Scriptures, concerning His Son, who was born of a descendant of David according to the flesh, who was declared the Son of God with power by the resurrection from the dead, according to the Spirit of holiness, Jesus Christ our Lord, (Romans 1:1-4), (also see 1John 2:2).*

Thus, the Resurrection of the Two Revelation Prophets will be God's "declaration" that the message they brought, and the judgment deeds they performed, were in total agreement with His Divine Will!

#1 God Is, And He Is Not Silent!

When you hear the word witness or witnesses, you should automatically think of a courtroom. Yes, the Judge is in His heavenly chambers, but the people in the courtroom do not see Him, so they pretend that He does not exist.

God is, and He is not silent, and He will send His two star witnesses to speak for Him. When God was giving the Law to Israel, the people did not want to hear "directly" from God for fear of death, so they requested that God send them Prophets instead of God's direct contact with them.

> *"The LORD your God will raise up for you a prophet like me from among you, from your countrymen, you shall listen to him. This is according to all that you asked of the LORD your God in Horeb on the day of the assembly, saying, 'Let me not hear again the voice of the LORD my God, let me not see this great fire anymore, lest I die.' The LORD said to me, 'They have spoken well. I will raise up a prophet from among their countrymen like you, and I will put My words in his mouth, and he shall speak to them all that I*

command him. It shall come about that whoever will not listen to My words which he shall speak in My name, I Myself will require it of him. But, the prophet who speaks a word presumptuously in My name which I have not commanded him to speak, or which he speaks in the name of other gods, that prophet shall die" (Deuteronomy 18:15-20).

Unfortunately, for the people in the courtroom, this heavenly Judge has already made His decision about their guilt.

"For God did not send the Son into the world to judge, the world, but that the world might be saved through Him. He who believes in Him (The Lord Jesus Christ) is not judged; he who does not believe has been judged already, because he has not believed in the name of the only begotten Son of God. This is the judgment, that the light has come into the world, and men loved the darkness rather than the light, for their deeds were evil. For everyone who does evil hates the light, and does not come to the light, for fear that his deeds will be exposed. But he who practices the truth comes to the light, so that his deeds may be manifested as having been wrought in God" (John 3:17-21).

The Judge makes the rules in His courtroom and enforces His regulations and standards. He requires obedience to His laws, and what He says goes, and you are guilty until proven innocent. *"All have sinned and fall short of the glory of God"*

(Romans 3:23). Manyother Witnesses/Prophets have already come and have given testimony, but these Two Revelation Prophets will arise and confirm the warnings and judgments of the Judge.

His judgments have already been affirmed, and the people of the world must get a high-powered defense attorney immediately.

> *""Make friends quickly with your opponent at law while you are with him on the way, in order that your opponent may not deliver you to the judge, and the judge to the officer, and you be thrown into prison. "Truly I say to you, you shall not come out of there, until you have paid up the last cent (Matt 5:25-26).*

The LORD Jesus Christ comes highly recommended because if one tries to defend himself, *"He has a fool for a client."* Again, the Judge will not even listen to their defenses and excuses.

> *"But these enemies of mine, who did not want me to reign over them, bring them here and slay them in my presence" (Luke 19:27).*

The Two Witnesses of Revelation will be witnesses for the prosecution against all humanity who are guilty of *high treason* against God's anointed King and His Kingdom. Note well that high treason carries with it the death penalty.

3

"But all these things they will do to you for My name's sake, because they do not know the One who sent Me. "If I had not come and spoken to them, they would not have sin, but now they have no excuse for their sin. He who hates Me hates My Father also. If I had not done among them the works which no one else did, they would not have sin; but now they have both seen and hated Me and My Father as well" (John 15:21-25).

The works Jesus did were to give the world a glimpse of the King and His Kingdom. However, even today, the world's people want nothing to do with the King or His Kingdom. They love the world and the kingdoms of this world that are fathered by their father, the Devil (1 John 2:15-17).

"And Jesus answered him, "It is written, 'MAN SHALL NOT LIVE BY BREAD ALONE." And the devil took Him up, and showed Him all the kingdoms of the world in a moment of time, and said to Him, "To You I will give all this authority and their glory; for it has been delivered to me, and I give it to whom I will. If You, then, will worship me, it shall all be Yours" (Luke 4:4-7 RSV).

"From the days of John the Baptist until now the kingdom of heaven suffers violence, and violent men take it by force" (Matt. 11:12); (see Matt. 21:33-46).

The people of the world demonstrate their rebellion to the Kingand His Kingdom by practicing lawlessness (breaking Kingdom Laws, statutes, and ordinances) and they do not give honor orreverence to the *Lord of lords and King of kings* (Revelation 17:14).

> *For even though they knew God, they did not honor Him as God, or give thanks; but they became futile intheir speculations, and their foolish heart was darkened (Romans 1:21).*

> *"There will be tribulation and distress for every soul of man who does evil, of the Jew first and also of the Greek, but glory and honor and peace to every man who does good, to the Jew first and also to the Greek. For there is no partiality with God" (Rom. 2:9).*

#2 ALL OF GOD'S PEOPLE ARE WITNESSES

Accordingly, in the case of the Two Revelation Witnesses, it is important that you listen to what they say, because what they do is only God's confirmation that they are speaking on His behalf. As such, the reader must compare their individual beliefs with the teachings of all of God's witnesses.

When the apostasy comes, those presently in Christendom willnot leave Christendom but will continue to believe in their false views as to what it means to be a Christian. They will reject the true gospel message as presented in the Scriptures and by the Two Revelation Witnesses. The wolves in sheep's clothing will not repentand they will continue to teach falsely. Those departing the true faith (the apostates) will not follow "The Antichrist" (at this point) because he does not come on the scene until after the testimony of the Two Witnesses has been completed.

All of God's people must understand that everyone in ministry has the same job description as the Two Revelation Witnesses. The first thing that one must realize is the fact that these Two Prophets are not independent of the other Biblical Prophets. Their authority to be witnesses is from the

Lord, which is the same authority given to all of God's people, which is the Word of God (see Matthew 28:18- 20). It will be like Moses said in Numbers chapter 11,

> *"But Moses said to him, "Are you jealous for my sake? Would that all the LORD's people were prophets, that the LORD would put His Spirit upon them!"* (Numbers 11:29).

> *"For you can all prophesy one by one, so that all may learn and all may be exhorted; and the spirits of prophets are subject to prophets; for God is not a God of confusion but of peace, as in all the churches of the saints"* (1 Corinthians 14:31-33).

These Two Prophets will be Two Servants (messengers) of God like all others called into ministry, but they will have the authority and be like the writing apostles in that they will not change the formerly written text. However, they will build on what the former writing Prophets themselves intended in their texts. They will clarify what has been written (e.g., Matthew 2:15, quoting Jeremiah 31:15; Corinthians 10:4; alluding to Exodus 17:6ff; and Galatians 4; looking back to Genesis 21).

The key is that these Two Prophets in The Book of Revelation will not give new Revelation. The Scriptures are complete with its sixty-six books; so these Two Prophets will only illuminate and carry out what is written. The Spirits of the Prophets are subject to the Prophets. So, these Two Prophets will only proclaim forth what is to come according to what has already been written. They will preach and expect repentance from their listeners (signified by the wearing of sackcloth and their judgment signs). Wake Up, Listen Up, or Go Down!

> *"And I will grant authority to my two witnesses, and they will prophesy for twelve hundred and sixty days, clothed in sackcloth"* (Revelation 11:3).

> *"Then He began to denounce the cities in which mostof His miracles were done, because they did not repent. "Woe to you, Chorazin! Woe to you, Bethsaida! For if the miracles had occurred in Tyre and Sidon which occurred in you, they would have repented long ago in sackcloth and ashes"* [Matthew 11:20-21 (Jesus speaking)].

These Two Prophets will Preach Repentance from Sin (telling the Repentant Ones to Sin no more) and for the Repentant Ones to bring Forth Fruit in keeping with that Repentance (that is for them to rectify the former evils they have done to others—if possible?) (e.g., Luke 19:1-10).

Preachers today are not teaching that part of the message. Example: What if a man had small children and ends up getting divorced but then believes? Would you tell him that he must pay his child support in keeping with his repentance? John theBaptist would say, "Yes!" (See Matthew 3:5-12).

> *"But if anyone does not provide for his own, andespecially for those of his household, he has*

denied the faith, and is worse than an unbeliever" (1 Timothy. 5:8).

That will be a test for the man to see if he loves his money more then he loves his wife and his children. If he fails the test, it shows that his faith was in vain. He was unable to bring forth fruit in keeping with his repentance. Thus, repentance for the forgiveness of sins should be preached by all of God's people, and His Two Revelation Witnesses will proclaim the same.

> *"Now He said to them, "These are My Words which I spoke to you while I was still with you, that all things which are written about Me in the Law of Moses and the Prophets and the Psalms must be fulfilled." Then He opened their minds to understand the Scriptures, and He said to them, "Thus it is written, that the Christ should suffer and rise again from the dead the third day, and that repentance for forgiveness of sins would be proclaimed in His name to all the nations, beginning from Jerusalem. You are witnesses of these things. And behold, I am sending forth the promise of My Father upon you; but you are to stay in the city until you are clothed with power from on high"* (Luke 24:44-49).

#3 THE UNITY OF ALL TRUE BELIEVERS

Only when you have the power of the Holy Spirit are you to preach His message with His power. The Spirit's uniting message toall is:

> *"Therefore I, the prisoner of the Lord, implore you to walk in a manner worthy of the calling with which you have been called, with all humility and gentleness, with patience, showing tolerance for one another in love, being diligent to preserve the unity of the Spirit in the bond of peace. There is one body and one Spirit, just as also you were called in one hope of your calling; one Lord, one faith, one baptism, one God and Father of all who is over alland through all and in all. But to each one of us gracewas given according to the measure of Christ's gift"* (Ephesians 4:1-7).

So, after repentance, all truly called "People of The Way" are to walk worthy of their calling with humility, gentleness, patience, showing forbearance to one another in love, and we are to preserve the unity of the Holy Spirit in the bond of peace.

This unity does not come from the combining of all religions or sects into one, but the unity is in the doctrinal teachings that there is only one Godly Truth, and that Truth is in The Person of the Lord Jesus Christ (The Living Word of God). *"Jesus said to him, "I am the way, and the truth, and the life; no one comes to the Father but through Me"* (John 14:6).

"But to each one of us, grace was given according to the measure of Christ's gift" (Ephesians 4:7). One may not have the Faith of the Two Prophets in the Book of Revelation (like the ability to move mountains), but God has given all His witnesses enough Grace and Faith to carry out their call to ministry. *"For we are His workmanship, created in Christ Jesus for good works, which God prepared beforehand, that we should walk in them"* (Ephesians 2:10).

You have to ask yourself, "What is the purpose of the Two Witnesses coming if they only have the same resources at their disposal as the rest of the Saints?" (The resources that all of God's Saints have at their disposal are the Holy Spirit, Prayer, Faith, and the Scriptures). Again, their purpose of coming is to proclaim the one True Faith and build up and encourage the people of The Way that believe in the faith that was once for all delivered to the Saints (Jude 3).

You are not to add to the Scriptures or take away from the Scriptures because truth combined with error is error (Mark 7:9-13).

"I testify to everyone who hears the words of the prophecy of this book: if anyone adds to them, God

will add to him the plagues which are written in this book; and if anyone takes away from the words of the book of this prophecy, God will take away his part from the tree of life and from the holy city, which are written in this book. He who testifies to these things says, "Yes, I am coming quickly." Amen. Come, Lord Jesus" (Revelation 22:18-20).

Jesus prayed that His Church of many members would be a united oneness, just like the oneness of the Trinity.

"I have given them Your word; and the world has hated them, because they are not of the world, even as I am not of the world. I do not ask You to take them out of the world, but to keep them from the evil one. They are not of the world, even as I am not of the world. Sanctify them in the truth; Your word is truth. As You sent Me into the world, I also have sent them into the world. For their sakes I sanctify Myself, that they themselves also may be sanctified in truth. I do not ask on behalf of these alone, but for those also who believe in Me through their word; that they may all be one; even as You, Father, are in Me, and I in You, that they also may be in Us, so that the world may believe that You sent Me. The glory which You have given Me I have given to them, that they may be one, just as We are one; I in them, and You in Me, that they may be perfected in unity, that the world may know that You sent

Me, and loved them, evenas You have loved Me"
(John 17:14-23).

This prayer is giving us our marching orders in the world. He has given us His Word, The Bible, that makes us holy (sanctified in the truth), but much of the preaching today is even against this prayer of Jesus. He prayed that the Father **would not take us out of the world** (like Pretribulation Preachers suggest). He prayed that the Father would keep us in the world, to be witnesses to the Son, and He also prayed that they would be protected from the evil one.

The Two Prophets are sent to answer Jesus' prayer of being perfected in unity, so the world will know that the Father loves His Son; and the Father will love those who love His Son.

The Church will be united by the one true faith as revealed in the Scriptures. The Church is presently divided with its Christian cults, sects, denominations, cultural Christians, lukewarm Christians, nominal Christians, and the like. So, the Two Witnesses are being sent to "unify" and "purify" His Church, and to preach the "united" Holiness of the Saints. The teaching of the Two Witnesses on Personal Holiness will have the "lip service professing Christians" reject this teaching in droves (thus, the continuing Apostasy).

#4 FALSE TEACHERS

The Two Prophets will help get rid of the chaff and tares from His True Church. They will also help get rid of those professing Christians who dishonor the name of the Lord Jesus Christ by their godless sinful behavior (their deeds). Yes, we are talking about those who call Jesus Lord, but do not do what He says (Luke 6:46).

The reality is that our churches are not being run by shepherds or cowboys, they are being lead by wolves who lord their ecclesiastical positions over the laity. The laity are being lorded over by the wolf packs. Yes, many of these wolves believe they are saved, and that they are children of God and they even profess Jesus as Lord, but they are deceived and deceiving.

At this point you are being advised to read Numbers 16 about the rebellion of Korah and his associates. Why? Because this type of rebellion (by the wolves) will happen in the future against the Prophets like Moses and Elijah.

Korah's rebellion was carried out by the liberal members of the congregation. Korah wanted to be part of the Aaronic Priesthood of which the Law prohibited him from being part. So, Korah gets political and gets some two hundred and fifty leaders of the congregation, chosen in the assembly, men of renown to protest the Laws limitation as to who can be priests. In fact Korah said to Moses, "You have gone far enough, for all the congregation are holy, every one of them, and the LORD is in their midst; so why do you exalt yourselves above the assembly of the LORD?" (Numbers 16:3). So, their argument was that all of the people in the congregation (including women) should be able to be priests. They were exerting political pressure on Moses to change the extremely limited restrictions about the Aaronic Priesthood.

So, what was the problem? Korah and his followers did not understand (believe) that the teachings about the Aaronic Priesthood were from God (they did not believe God nor fear God). They thought it was Moses exalting himself above the assembly of the LORD. They believed their political protest would make Moses change his mind and his teachings. Unfortunately, Moses could not and would not change God's teachings. Moses wanted Korah and his liberal followers to understand that the judgments that were coming upon them were not his doing. It was a result of their rebellion against the LORD'S teachings. Moses says, "By this you shall know that the LORD has sent me to do all these deeds; for this is not my doing (It is the LORD'S doing) (Numbers 16:28). All that Moses was doing was from the LORD and even the things that happened to those protesting groups happened because they had spurned the LORD.

In the future the liberal elements of Christianity will say that the teaching of the LORD'S Two Witnesses are too narrowly interpreted. They will try to get the Two Prophets to be more liberal in their interpretation but like Moses and Aaron they could not and will not change the LORD'S teachings.

One of the Laws of Kingdom Living is not to curse God or curse a ruler of your people. The Two Prophets in The Book of the Revelation are not to be cursed. This is important for us today because it is God's teaching and they can not change what has been written. The critics will be arguing in favor of the sin nature and how sin should be tolerated, but there is no way they can win that argument with God. But their stated position on being "sinners" saved by grace speaks volumes about their father, the Devil (John 8:43-47).

> *"For it is written, 'You shall not speak evil of a ruler of your people"* (Acts 23:5).

Thus, a warning to the world's secular and religious leaders. If you speak evil against those Two Prophets, you will be rebelling andspeaking against God. Remember, what also happened to Miriam who spoke against Moses. The key is that no one should speak evil of a ruler of the people (and that prohibition includes Presidents).

> *"With him (Moses) I speak mouth to mouth, even openly, and not in dark sayings, and he beholds the form of the LORD. Why then were*

you not afraid to speak against My servant, against Moses?" (Numbers 12:8).

Yes, Miriam, you should have been afraid to speak against your brother Moses, the Prophet of God. It will also be the loud and the proud wolves who do not fear man nor God and will speak against the Two Prophets and they will criticize things they do not know or understand. It is the wolves who will do the most grumbling and complaining.

> *"But these men revile the things which they do not understand; and the things which they know by instinct, like unreasoning animals, by these things they are destroyed. Woe to them! For they have gone the way of Cain, and for pay they have rushed headlong into the error of Balaam, and perished in the rebellion of Korah. These men are those who are hidden reefs in your love feasts when they feast with you without fear, caring for themselves; clouds without water, carried along by winds; autumn trees without fruit, doubly dead, uprooted; wild waves of the sea, casting up their own shame like foam; wandering stars, for whom the black darkness has been reserved forever"* (Jude 10-13).

Remember, many people think it is a God-given right to grumble and complain, but it is just the opposite. God wants you to be thankful for everything (1 Thessalonians 5:18) and stop your grumbling and complaining. Many will not make it into heaven, because God knows they would continue to do their grumbling and complaining even in heaven. So, why did Korah and his followers perish? Well, he (Korah) was not satisfied with the position or role that God planned for him, he pridefully felt that he was greater than just being a servant. He wanted to be a "Recognized Leader!"

> *"Then Moses said to Korah, "Hear now, you sons of Levi, is it not enough for you that the God of Israel has separated you from the rest of the congregation of Israel, to bring you near to Himself, to do the service of the tabernacle of the Lord, and to stand before the congregation to minister to them; and that He has brought you near, Korah, and all your brothers, sons of Levi, with you? And are you seeking for the priesthood also? "Therefore you and all your company are gathered together against the LORD; but as for Aaron, who is he that you grumble against him?"* (Numbers 16:8-11).

Moses would say to Korah, "You are not grumbling and complaining against me or Aaron, you are grumbling against the LORD. So, if anyone grumbles against God's Revelation Witnesses, they would be grumbling against God, and that does not go over well with God. Moses is critical of the charges brought against him and Aaron by Korah and associates. Moses would say something like this to Korah, "So, you are not content "with the role that God has given you" to serve in the tabernacle; thus, this disturbance of yours is rebellion against God.

Nor let us try the Lord, as some of them did, and were destroyed by the serpents. Nor grumble, as some of them did, and were destroyed by the destroyer. Now these things happened to them as an example, and they were written for our instruction, upon whom the ends of the ages have come (1 Corinthians 10:9-11).

"Beware of the false prophets, who come to you in sheep's clothing, but inwardly are ravenous wolves… Not everyone who says to Me, 'Lord, Lord,' will enter the kingdom of heaven, but he who does the will of My Father who is in heaven will enter. Many will say to Me on that day, 'Lord, Lord, did we not prophesy in Your name, and in Your name cast out demons, and in Your name perform many miracles?' And then I will declare to them, 'I never knew you; DEPART FROM ME, YOU WHO PRACTICE LAWLESSNESS" (Matthew 7:15; 21-23).

These false teachers are wolves in sheep's clothing (under the umbrella of Christendom).

"And Jesus answered and said to them, "See to it that no one misleads you. "For many will come in My name, saying, 'I am the Christ,' and will mislead many" (Matthew 24:4-5).

Yes, they call Jesus Lord and say that He is the Christ, but they will mislead many. However, what gives them away?

They continue to practice sinful behavior (lawlessness). *"And then I will declare to them, 'I never knew you; DEPART FROM ME, YOU WHO PRACTICE LAWLESSNESS"* (Matthew 7:23).

Their lawlessness is deplorable, but their teachings are even more despicable because their followers are taught that they cannot and will not get the victory over sin while here on Earth. Thus, denying the finished work of the Lord Jesus Christ on the cross. The sin nature is sin, and for one to say that Jesus Christ's death on the cross did not cleanse us from all our sin, then that teaching is blasphemous.

> *"For by one offering **He has perfected** for all time those who are sanctified"* (Heb 10:14).

> *"If we confess our sins, he is faithful and righteous to forgive us our sins and to cleanse us from all unrighteousness"* (1 John 1:9-10).

> They teach that Paul was a sinner even after being saved!

This teaching is not only false teaching, but it is blasphemous teaching as well. They make Paul out to be a sinner like themselves rather than the Saint that he was. Paul had to defend his Apostleship against the false teachers of his day; but today, he would have to defend even his Sainthood against today's false teachers.

What does that mean to the faithful Saints of God? If they say that Paul continued to be a sinner after being saved, then what chance do you have of convincing them that you are a born-again Saint, one of the righteous ones, a holy one, one who is pure in heart and perfect?

In Romans chapter seven, Paul talks about himself as an unsaved person. Anyone who has ever been brought up under the Law understands Paul's frustration of not being able to do what he knew he should do to keep the Law.

> *"For the good that I wish, I do not do; but I practicethe very evil that I do not wish. But if I am doing the very thing I do not wish, I am no longer the one doingit, but sin which dwells in me. I find then the principlethat evil (sin) is present in me, the one who wishes todo good"* (Romans 7:19-21).

This is what James would say about what Paul said:

> *"Therefore, to one who knows the right thing to do, and does not do it, to him it is sin"* (James 4:17).

That is what Paul was saying, "Before I became a Believer in The Lord Jesus Christ I was a hypocrite like all non-believers.

> *"But if I do the very thing I do not want to do, I agree with the Law, confessing that the Law is good. So now, no longer am I the one doing it, but* **sin** *which dwells me. For I know that* **nothing good dwells in me**, *that is, in my flesh; for the willing is present in me, but the doing of the good is not"* (Romans 7:16-18).

Paul is saying that the sin nature that was presently indwelling him prevented him from doing the good that he wanted to do. He wanted to do good but was unable to do so. That is the testimony of an unsaved person who is a slave to sin. Verse 17 and 18 above says, "*but sin which dwells in me. For I know that nothing good dwells in me, that is, in my flesh.*" Yes, Paul nothing good dwells in you as a non-believer, but let us look at what you said later as a Believer:

> "*However, you are not in the flesh but in the Spirit, if indeed the* **Spirit of God dwells in you**. *But if anyone does not have the Spirit of Christ, he does not belong to Him. If Christ is in you, though the body is dead because of sin, yet the spirit is alive because of righteousness.* **But if the Spirit of Him who raised Jesus from the dead dwells in you,** *He who raised Christ Jesus from the dead will also give life to your mortal bodies through His Spirit who indwells you*" (Roman 8:9-11).

So, in chapter 7, Paul says nothing good dwells in him and here in chapter 8, he says the Spirit of Him who raised Jesus from the dead dwells in him and in all Believers. So, the no-good thing in chapter 7 is sin, but having the Spirit of God in chapter 8 is a good thing. If anyone does not have the Spirit of Christ, he does not belong to Him. Paul had the Spirit of God in him, and he was now a Saint and not a sinner.

> "*Paul, called as an apostle of Jesus Christ by the will of God, and Sosthenes our brother, To the church of God which is at Corinth, **to those who***

have been sanctified in Christ Jesus, saints by calling, with all who in every place call on the name of our Lord Jesus Christ, their Lord and ours: Grace to you and peace from God our Father and the Lord Jesus Christ" (1 Corinthians 1:1-3).

*"Jesus presented another parable to them, saying, 'The kingdom of heaven may be compared to a man who sowed good seed in his field. **But while men were sleeping, his enemy came and sowed tares also among the wheat and went away.** But when the wheat sprouted and bore grain, then the tares became evident also.' The slaves of the landowner came and said to him, 'Sir, did you not sow good seed in your field? How then does it have tares?' And he said to them, 'An enemy has done this!' The slaves said to him, 'Do you want us, then, to go and gather them up?' But he said, 'No; lest while you are gathering up the tares, you may root up the wheat with them. Allow both to grow together until the harvest; and in the time of the harvest I will say to the reapers, "First gather up the tares and bind them in bundles to burn them up; but gather the wheat into my barn"* (Matthew 13:24-30).

The key to this parable is the fact that the men of the kingdom were sleeping, and the enemy came and sowed tares among us, and we kept on sleeping. It was like Jesus in the garden when He wanted his disciples to stay awake.

> *"And He came and found them sleeping, and said to Peter, "Simon, are you asleep? Could you not keep watch for one hour? Keep watching and praying, that you may not come into temptation; the spirit is willing, but the flesh is weak. Again He went away and prayed, saying the same words. And again He came and found them sleeping, for their eyes were very heavy;* **and they did not know what to answer Him.** *And He came the third time, and said to them, "Are you still sleeping and taking your rest? it is enough; the hour has come; behold, the Son of Man is being betrayed into the hands of sinners. "Get up, let us be going; behold, the one who betrays Me is at hand!"* (Mark 14:37-42).

Wake Up, Listen Up, or Go Down!

> *"Children, it is the last hour; and just as you heard that Antichrist is coming, even now many antichrists have appeared; from this we know that it is the last hour. They went out from us; but they were not really of us; for if they had been of us; they would have remained with us; but they went out, so that it would be shown that they all are not of us. But you have an anointing from the Holy One, and you all know"* (1 John 2:18-21).

The false teachers have put the Saints to sleep, and Christ's True Church has to wake up. Sleeping beauty has to kiss the Son (Psalm 2:12, NIV) and remember what He promised you before you ate of the poisonous teachings of the wolves.

> *"Do not let your heart be troubled; believe in God, believe also in Me. In My Father's house are many dwelling places; if it were not so, I would have told you; for I go to prepare a place for you. "If I go and prepare a place for you, I will come again, and receive you to Myself, that where I am, there you may be also"* (John 14:1-3).

Jesus states, I'm coming for my bride very shortly, and I want her to be awake and ready for My arrival so that we can live "Happily Ever After" (Revelation 1:3 and Revelation 22:20-21). However, while you are still in the body you must live above reproach and expose the wolves for their false, blasphemous teachings.

> *"As I urged you upon my departure for Macedonia, remain on at Ephesus, so that you may instruct certain men not to teach strange doctrines, nor to pay attention to myths and endless genealogies, which give rise to mere speculation rather than furthering the administration of God which is by faith. But the goal of our instruction is love from a pure heart and a good conscience and a sincere faith. For some men, straying from these things, have turned aside to fruitless discussion, wanting to be teachers of the Law, even though*

they do not understand either what they are saying or the matters about which they make confident assertions. But we know that the Law is good, if one uses it lawfully, realizing the fact that Law is not made for a righteous person, but for those who are lawless and rebellious, for the ungodly and sinners, for the unholy and profane, for those who kill their fathers or mothers, for murderers and immoral men and homosexuals and kidnappers and liars and perjurers, and whatever else is contrary to sound teaching, according to the glorious gospel of the blessed God, with which I have been entrusted" (1 Timothy 1:3-11).

Many of those who will depart from the faith will be the lukewarm people who did not and will not repent of their godless deeds.

"To the angel of the church in Laodicea write: "The Amen, the faithful and true Witness, the Beginning of the creation of God, says this: 'I know your deeds, that you are neither cold nor hot; I would that you were cold or hot. So because you are lukewarm, and neither hot nor cold, I will spit you out of My mouth. Because you say, "I am rich, and have become wealthy, and have need of nothing," and you do not know that you are wretched and miserable and poor and blind and naked, I advise you to buy from Me gold refined by fire, that you may become rich, and

white garments, so that you may clothe yourself, and that the shame of your nakedness may not be revealed; and eye salve to anoint your eyes, so that you may see" (Revelation 3:14-22).

If you recognize yourself in the above scriptures, you can repent because the door is still wide open.

#5 YOUR CALL TO HOLINESS

"Those whom I love, I reprove and discipline; be zealous therefore, and repent. 'Behold, I stand at the door and knock; if anyone hears My voice and opens the door, I will come in to him, and will dine with him, and he with Me. He who overcomes, I will grant to him to sit down with Me on My throne, as I also overcame and sat down with My Father on His throne. He who has an ear, let him hear what the Spirit says to the churches" (Revelation 3:19-22).

The most important thing one has to understand is that judgment starts with the household of God. Yes, God's judgments do not end at His household, but they do start there! That is the main reason that the Two Prophets are coming --- to Judge the Household of God. The argument of those who do not obey the Gospel of God would be asking, "Why doesn't God straighten out His household before He tries to straighten out the rest of us? That is exactly what God is going to do. He is going to straighten out His household by spitting them out of His mouth and then will come "The Day of the Lord Judgments" on all of them.

"For it is time for judgment to begin with the household of God; and if it begins with us first, what will be the outcome for those who do not obey the gospel of God? AND IF IT IS WITH DIFFICULTY THAT THE RIGHTEOUS IS SAVED, WHAT WILL BECOME OF THE GODLESS MAN AND THE SINNER? Therefore, let those also who suffer according to the will of God entrust their souls to a faithful Creator in doing what is right" (1 Peter 4:17-19).

God always warns before He destroys, and those two Revelation Prophets are God's final warning before, "The Day of the Lord" starts. They will preach repentance, righteous and holy living. That is why there will be resistance to them from the wolves in sheep's clothing. Those wolves will say like the world's people say, "Nobody's Perfect," but if you are not holy (sanctified and perfect) you will not see God.

"Blessed are the pure in heart, for they shall see God" (Matthew 5:8). *"Pursue peace with all men, and the sanctification without which no one will see the Lord"* (Hebrews12:14).

There are two false statements that most people make and they both start with the word "Nobody." The two false statementsare, "Nobody's Perfect" and the other is "Nobody Knows for Sure." For those who say, *"Nobody's Perfect"* they better read what God said in the Scriptures about Job and Noah:

> *"And the LORD said unto Satan, hast thou considered My servant Job, that there is none like him in the earth, a perfect and an upright man, one that feareth God, and escheweth evil? And still he holdeth fast his integrity, although thou movedst Me against him, to destroy him without cause"* (Job 2:3 KJV).

> *"This is the generations of Noah. Noah was a just man, perfect in his generations, and Noah walked with God"* (Genesis 6:9 KJV).

> *"Surely God is good to Israel, to those who are pure in heart!"* (Psalms 73:1).

Today's professing Christians talk about Progressive Sanctification (Progressive Holiness), but sanctification is not progressive. You are holy, or you are defiled. You are in the light or you are in the darkness. You cannot become more holy than holy. If you are separated from sin, you are holy, but if you are a sinner, you are defiled. You cannot be almost holy or almost undefiled. Holiness is purity and purity is perfection, and that is why God's Holy Ones are holy, pure in heart, and perfect.

> *"To the pure, all things are pure; but to those who are defiled and unbelieving, nothing is pure, but both their mind and their conscience are defiled. They profess to know God, but by their deeds they deny Him, being detestable and*

disobedient, and worthless for any good deed"
(Titus 1:15-16).

Purity is 100 percent free from any impurities or contaminants (like pure gold), but sin makes one impure, and it debases, contaminates and pollutes. What the above verses are saying is that the Saints (the Holy Ones who are the Pure in Heart) cannot do anything wrong in the eyes of our Father, but the disobedient detestable, and worthless ones cannot do anything right.

Many professing Christians have a problem with the word "perfect." However, to be holy means to be without sin, and if you are without sin, then you are perfected in holiness in God's sight, and He is the only person that matters. According to the world's people (who consistently judge falsely according to appearances) who say, "Nobody is righteous, holy and perfect, they are including The Lord Jesus Christ Himself" in that false statement. However, even sinful Herod recognized that John the Baptist was a righteous and holy man:

> *"Herodias had a grudge against him and wanted to put him to death and could not do so; for Herod was afraid of John, knowing that he was a righteous and holy man, and kept him safe. And when he heardhim, he was very perplexed; but he used to enjoy listening to him"* (Mark 6:19-20).

Yes, one should fear the righteous because of what they say and have no fear of the unrighteous. Jesus said in Matthew

5:48, *"Therefore you are to be perfect, as your heavenly Father is perfect."*

Jesus is here giving a command and not a suggestion. Perfection is the standard. If you break even one of God's Laws, youare less than perfect and defiled, and you will be judged as a sinner. *"Behold, all souls are Mine; the soul of the father as well as the soul of the son is mine. The soul who sins will die"* (Ezekiel 18:4).

It is the Lord who determines your position with Him and not men. The following is what Paul said about himself and the peopleof God:

> *"Let a man regard us in this manner, as servants of Christ, and stewards of the mysteries of God. In this case, moreover, it is required of stewards that one be found trustworthy. **But to me it is a very small thing that I may be examined by you, or by any human court; in fact, I do not even examine myself.** For I am conscious of nothing against myself, yet I am not by this acquitted; but the one who examines me is the Lord. Therefore do not go on passing judgment before the time, but wait until the Lord comes who will both bring to light the things hidden in the darkness and disclose the motives of men's hearts; and then each man's praise will come to him from God"* (1 Corinthians 4:1-5).

"Who are you to judge the servant of another? To his own master he stands or falls; and stand he will, for the Lord is able to make him stand" (Romans 14:4).

The second false statement that many people make is that, "Nobody Knows for Sure." Oh!, "The People of The Way, "Know for Sure! In fact if you do not "Know for Sure" than you do not have a True Saving Faith. The reason that God has given us His Holy Spirit and His Scriptures is to tell us that we can, "Know for Sure!"

These things I have written to you who believe in the name of the Son of God, in order that you may know that you have eternal life (1 John 5:13).

Many other signs therefore Jesus also performed in the presence of the disciples, which are not written in this book; but these have been written that you may believe that Jesus is the Christ, the Son of God; and that believing you may have life in His name (John 20:30-31).

Yes, the resistance will come from the people of the world, but more will even come from the false teachers "The wolves in sheep's clothing." Meaning, some of the most significant resistance andpersecution of the Saints will come from those professing Christians that say Jesus is Lord, but they do not do what He says.

"And Jesus answered and said to them, "See to it that no one misleads you. "For many will come in My name, saying, 'I am the Christ,' and will mislead many" (Matthew 24:4-5).

These false teachers come in the name of the Lord; they call themselves Christians, and even say that Jesus is the Christ, but be warned because many of them are deceivers. Yes, they have the "form of godliness," but they deny the power that God gives His real children for overcoming the sinful works of the Devil.

"But realize this, that in the last days difficult times will come. For men will be lovers of self, lovers of money, boastful, arrogant, revilers, disobedient to parents, ungrateful, unholy, unloving, irreconcilable, malicious gossips, without self-control, brutal, haters of good, treacherous, reckless, conceited, lovers of pleasure rather than lovers of God; holding to a form of godliness, although they have denied its power; and avoid such men as these" (2 Timothy 3:1-5).

What power have they denied? The power that God gives to His people to overcome sin and the works of the Devil.

"Little children let no one deceive you; the one who practices righteousness is righteous, just as He is righteous; the one who practices sin is of the devil; for the devil has sinned from the beginning. The Son of God appeared for this purpose, that

He might destroy the works of the devil" (1 John 3:7-8).

They deny God's power because they do not have the Holy Spirit's ability to stop doing the evil things mentioned above in

1. Timothy 3:1-5.

    "But you, beloved, ought to remember the words that were spoken beforehand by the apostles of our Lord Jesus Christ, that they were saying to you, 'In the last time there shall be mockers, following after their own ungodly lusts.' These are the ones who cause divisions, worldly-minded, devoid of the Spirit" (Jude 17-19).

The *wolves in sheep's clothing* disguise themselves as being sheep (Christians) but they are deceiving, backbiting sheep killers at heart. Our church leaders are not fulfilling the marching orders God has given to them for maturing the people of God.

    "And He gave some as apostles, and some as prophets, and some as evangelists, and some as pastors and teachers, for the equipping of the saints for the work of service, to the building up of the body of Christ" (Ephesians 4:11-12).

So, everyone who is called into service by God (including the Two Prophets) are there for equipping the Saints (The Holy Ones)for the work of service. So, what is your first order or first work of service? To become a Saint and then act like a Saint (A Holy One). Therefore, your are to prepare other Holy Ones for service. However, to do that, you must be holy yourself. Like Paul, we must be imitators of Christ (see 1 Corinthians 11:1).

In 1 Peter 2:9-10, Peter writes:

> *"But you are A CHOSEN RACE, A ROYAL PRIESTHOOD, A HOLY NATION, A PEOPLE FOR GOD'S OWN POSSESSION, that you may proclaim the excellencies of Him who has called you out of darkness into His marvelous light; for you once were NOT A PEOPLE, but now you are THE PEOPLE OF GOD; you had NOT RECEIVED MERCY, but now you have RECEIVED MERCY" (1 Peter 2:9-10).*

So, to be a Holy Nation of People, you must be made holy by your God who is Holy. As such, you not only receive the Holy Spirit, but God gives you a transformed mind (new thinking) and a new pure heart. So now your body, mind, and spirit are a living and holy sacrifice to God.

> *"Therefore, I urge you therefore, brethren, by the mercies of God, to present your bodies a living and holy sacrifice, acceptable to God, which is your spiritual service of worship. And do not be conformed to this world, but be transformed by the renewing of your mind, that you may prove*

what the will of God is, that which is good and acceptable and perfect" (Romans 12:1-2).

No, the body of a Believer is not sinful. The body of a saved person is the temple of the Holy Spirit, and your temple is no longer empty, nor is it defiled by the sin nature. You are no longer in Adam (having the sin nature), you are in Christ (having the life-giving Spirit, the divine nature). (1 Corinthians 15:45).

"For by these He has granted to us His precious and magnificent promises, so that by them you might become partakers of the divine nature, having escaped the corruption that is in the world by lust" (2 Peter 1:4).

As a believer, you are a new creature in Christ. That old sin nature has passed away. You are no longer a slave to sin. That is the power you receive at salvation, the power over sin. If you still have the sin nature, then you are by nature a child of wrath.

"Among them we too all formerly lived in the lusts of our flesh, indulging the desires of the flesh and of the mind, and were by nature children of wrath, even as the rest" (Ephesians 2:3).

But realize this, that in the last days difficult times will come. For men will be lovers of self, lovers of money, boastful, arrogant, revilers, disobedient to parents, ungrateful, unholy,

> *unloving, irreconcilable, malicious gossips, without*
> *self-control, brutal, haters of good, treacherous,*
> *reckless, conceited, lovers of pleasure rather than*
> *lovers of God; holding to a form of godliness,*
> *although they have denied its power; avoid such*
> *men as these* (2 Timothy 3:1-5).

If you continue to sin, it proves you still love yourself more than you love God and you prove yourself to be a lying hypocrite.

> *"We know that no one who is born of God sins;*
> *but he who was born of God keeps him and the*
> *evil one does not touch him. We know that we are*
> *of God, and the whole world lies in the power of*
> *the evil one. And we know that the Son of God has*
> *come, and has given us understanding, in order*
> *that we might know Him who is true, and we are*
> *in Him who is true, in His Son Jesus Christ. This*
> *is the true God and eternal life. Little children,*
> *guard yourselves from idols"* (1 John 5:18-21).

You who have been born again are direct creations of God (sons of God --- Romans 8:14), and you are no longer in Adam. Did you ever wonder why angels are called sons of God? (Job 1:6) Angels are also direct creations of God; they do not have a mother; they were direct creations by God. The people of God who are born again are also direct creations of God. Thus, both angels and Born Again Believers are the sons of God.

"That which is born of the flesh is flesh, and that which is born of the Spirit is spirit. "Do not marvel that I said to you, 'You must be born again'" (John 3:6)

Those in Adam are flesh, but those born of the Spirit are spirit.

"I have given them Thy word; and the world has hated them, because they are not of the world, even as I am not of the world" (John 17:14 KJV).

So, when you tell anyone (even professing Christians) that you are a True Disciple of the Lord Jesus Christ and you are like Him and not of this world, they will think you are a prideful boaster, and as such you will be persecuted. Then, when you say that you are righteous, holy, and perfect, as your Lord, their teeth (fangs) come out. They act like the wolf in the story of Little Red Riding Hood. "O Granny, what (a big mouth you are) and what big teeth you've got!

Moreover, the wolf replies, "All the better to eat you with, my dear!"

"Truly, I say to you, among those born of women there has not arisen anyone greater than John the Baptist; yet he who is least in the kingdom of heaven is greater than he. "And from the days of John the Baptist until now the kingdom of heaven suffers violence, and violent men take it by force" (Matt.1:11).

The wolves in sheep's clothing are violent men who try to take the kingdom by force, but it is the meek who will inherit the Earth.

> *"Truly I say to you, whoever does not receive the kingdom of God like a child shall not enter it at all."*

> *And He took them in His arms and began blessing them, laying His hands upon them"* (Mark 10:15-16).

> *"Which one of you convicts Me of sin? If I speak truth, why do you not believe Me? "He who is of God hears the words of God; for this reason you do not hear them, because you are not of God"* (John 8:46- 47 Jesus speaking).

Are you of God, and do you hear the words of God?

> *"The world cannot hate you* (Jesus to His unbelieving half-brothers); *but it hates Me because I testify of it, that its deeds are evil"* (John 7:7).

The people of God now worship God in their bodies and serve both God and their fellow man. When your thinking and your behavior are in sync, you are not a hypocrite, thus proving what the will of God is in your life (which is your sanctification, your holiness, and your purity).

> *For you know what commandments we gave you by the authority of the Lord Jesus. For this*

*is the will of God, your sanctification; that is,
that you abstain from sexual immorality; that
each of you know how topossess his own vessel in
sanctification and honor, not in lustful passion,
like the Gentiles who do not know God; and that
no man transgress and defraud his brother in
the matter because the Lord is the avenger in all
these things, just as we also told you before and
solemnly warned you. For God has not called us
for the purpose of impurity, but in sanctification.
Consequently, he who rejects this is not rejecting
man but the God who gives His Holy Spirit to you"*
(1 Thessalonians 4:2-8).

God wants each member of His body to be holy unto the
Lord.

*As obedient children, do not be conformed
to the former lusts which were yours in your
ignorance, but like the Holy One who called you,
be holy yourselves also in all your behavior; because
it is written, "YOU SHALL BE HOLY, FOR I
AM HOLY"* (1 Peter 1:14- 16).

Today, most evangelist, pastors, and teachers do not
live holy lives, and they do not even claim to be holy. They
believe they still have the sin nature (which they do), and as
such, some of God's people are following these false teachers
because they have been put to sleep (lacking discernment)
and they continue to sleep because they are not reading the
word of God for themselves. The only way one knows if

one is following a false teacher or not is by comparing their teachings, their lives, and their followers with the written word of God.

The false teachers keep on teaching that the Saints still have the sin nature, which is their excuse for their sinful actions (lawlessness - Matthew chapter 7). Thus, when you catch them openly sinning in any way (like having a so-called love child), they say, "We are all sinners, aren't we?" No, you are a hypocrite who is teaching falsely because, "The True People of God" - are Holy and Worship God in their bodies.

> *"Flee immorality. Every other sin that a man commits is outside the body, but the immoral man sins against his own body"* (1 Corinthians 6:18).

So, if someone teaches that the people of The Way still have the sin nature; are they false teachers or are they just victims of the false teachers?" Christendom is a big umbrella, and many who teach we still have the sin nature, are false teachers, but some (a small minority) let themselves be led and get intimidated by their false cult teachers.

The people of God are to humble themselves (James 4:10), but false teachers try to humiliate anyone and everyone who believes in and teaches present-day sanctification. These false teachers are like the college professors who try to intimidate their students by saying, "No intellectual person that I know believes in the Bible," and these wolves in sheep's clothing say, "I do not know anyone righteous, holy, and perfect!" Someone has to tell these people that they better get to know more people and especially the people of The Way. These false teachers are also like their father, the Devil, who quote the Scriptures out of context. They do that in order to try and shut up the holy ones. The following verses are examples of their out of context teachings.

"If we say that we have no sin, we are deceiving ourselves, and the truth is not in us" (1 John 1:8).

They say this verse and others that follow are talking about us (the holy ones), but these verses are talking about the *"sayers"*. John is saying throughout his epistle that the children of God are the doers, but the *sayers* are all talk and no action. (see 1 John 1:6, 8, 10 and 1 John 2:4,6,9).

There is a saying among the Saints, "If you cannot walk the walk, then do not talk the talk." So, if one has never read the Bible, and has never been convicted of sin by the Law, they would "say" something foolish like, "We have no sin," and in fact, they would foolishly continue to say that, "We have never sinned!"

"If we say that we have not sinned, we make Him a liar, and His word is not in us" (1 John 1:10).

These *sayers* (talkers) are the liars. The true people of God admit that they were sinners, but no longer, because they have been forgiven and cleansed from all unrighteousness.

"If we confess our sins, He is faithful and righteous to forgive us our sins and to cleanse us

43

from all unrighteousness. If we say that we have
not sinned (in the past), we make Him a liar, and
His word is not in us" (1 John 1:9-10).

He cleanses us from all unrighteousness. Yes, we were (past tense) sinners like the rest, but God….

"And you were dead in your trespasses and sins,
in which you formerly walked according to the
course of this world, according to the prince of the
power of the air, of the spirit that is now working
in the sons of disobedience. Among them we too all
formerly lived in the lusts of our flesh, indulging
the desires of the flesh and of the mind, and were
by nature children of wrath, even as the rest. But
God," (Ephesians 2:1).

So why do some of God's True Children believe and teach falsely? Because they do not follow the Spirit's teachings, but the teachings of men. (NB, All religious systems are controlled by Satan – the god of this world) [to be discussed later].

Today's People of The Way have not been properly exposedto the Biblical Teaching of present-day sanctification, because the false teachers mock and scoff at that teaching. The false teachers mock and scoff at God's people who believe in present-day sanctification, so as a result, many of the Saints have been intimidated and lulled to sleep by the false teachers.

Plus, the vast majority of people in Christendom have bought into the world's thinking, that man is basically good. However, nobody is perfect! These false teachers do not confront sinful behavior (like Jesus, John the Baptist and the other Prophets did). They make excuses for sinful behavior. E.g., Alcoholism is not the fault of the alcoholic; it is a disease. They will always find something or someone else to blame for their sinful dysfunctional lives. The something else that these false teachers blame for their sinful actions is the sin nature, and the *somebody* else is ultimately God?

What did Adam and Eve do after they sinned? They hid and then made excuses for their disobedient actions. To confess means to say the same thing about yourself and your actions that God says about you. A good confession is without excuses. Thus, Adam and Eve did not make a good confession. Eve blamed the Devil, and Adam blamed God.

> *"The man said, "The woman whom Thou gave to be with me, she gave me from the tree, and I ate." Then the LORD God said to the woman, "What is this you have done?" and the woman said, "The serpent deceived me, and I ate"* (Genesis 3:12-13).

So, who are the sin nature people blaming when they sin? The same ones that both Adam and Eve blamed, God and the Devil. Why God? Because they are saying, "God, you did not give us or anyone else (including your Holy Ones) enough power to overcome sin (the works of the Devil)." Therefore, God, it is your fault when we continue to sin?

45

Now that is what we call false teaching and playing the "blame game." Their distorted thinking continues something like this: "The excuses that Adam and Eve gave were pretty good, so we will follow their lead. "The Devil made me do it, and if you, God, would have destroyed the Devil at the beginning (like we advised You to do) we would not be sinning and having all these problems in the world. Therefore, "Our sinning is your fault God."

They continue to say, "We will not take personal responsibility for anything we say or do, because ever since Adam and Eve created/invented these good excuses, none of us are wrong.

So, if someone told you, they were *"sinners" saved by grace,* would you let them be your financial advisers? Why not? Most likely because when they steal your money, they will come back and say, "I told you I was a sinner (a thief) so why are you surprised and shocked to hear that I stole your money?" So, if you wouldn't hire a thief to handle your money, then why would you ever think of listening to a self confessed (lying) sinning preacher. You would be better off staying home and reading the words of the righteous in the Scriptures than to listen to an unrighteous self confessed lying sinner. The unrighteous have nothing to offer you but empty promises that they cannot fulfill. They are clouds without water, giving you empty promises.

> *"Woe to them! For they have gone the way of Cain, and for pay they have rushed headlong into theerror of Balaam, and perished in the rebellion*

of Korah. These are men who are hidden reefs in your love feasts when they feast with you without fear, caring for themselves; clouds without water, carried along by winds; autumn trees without fruit, doubly dead, uprooted;" (Jude 11-12)

You are to come out from among them and be separate says the Lord.

"Do not be bound together with unbelievers; for what partnership have righteousness and lawlessness, or what fellowship has light with darkness? Or what harmony has Christ with Belial, or what has a believer in common with an unbeliever? Or what agreement has the temple of God with idols? For we are the temple of the living God; just as God said, "I WILL DWELL IN THEM AND WALK AMONG THEM; AND I WILL BE THEIR GOD, AND THEY SHALL BE MY PEOPLE. "THEREFORE, COME OUT FROM THEIR MIDST AND BE SEPARATE," SAYS THE LORD. "AND DO NOT TOUCH WHAT IS UNCLEAN; and I will welcome you.

"And I will be a Father to you, and you shall be sons and daughters to Me," Says the Lord Almighty" (2 Corinthians 6:14-18).

These false teachers try to get at eye level with their sinning followers. Saying, "I am a sinner like you, and I feel your pain" and "I know what you are going through." "I've been there, and I've done that." However, in reality, they are both standing in the muck and mire of sinful behavior. Each one comforting the other saying, "This place where we are standing is not that bad, because one could easily get used to these corrupt surroundings and live with that putrid stench. "Whereas, the righteous do not go down in the muck and mire. They stand on the solid foundation and are willing to reach down and help them get on the solid rock, but they will not join them in their sinful pleasures.

> *"And in all this, they are surprised that you do not run with them into the same excess of dissipation, and they malign you; but they shall give account to Him who is ready to judge the living and the dead"*(1 Peter 4:4-5).

We have already talked about the unity of the faith, so why are not all Christian churches united in the once for all faith delivered to the Saints?

> *"For certain persons have crept in unnoticed, those who were long beforehand marked out for this condemnation, ungodly persons who turn the grace of our God into licentiousness and deny our only master and Lord, Jesus Christ"* (Jude 4 [Jude's answer is false teachers]).

The answer is false teachers. Yes, they call themselves Christians (but they are wolves in sheep's clothing and soul killers), many of them do not believe in or even teach the Law or sin. Theydo not even preach or practice Biblical Morality themselves or even practical Christian Ethical Standards. Many of them think that Christianity is a paycheck (a job), and Christianity is just one of the many philosophies of life. They believe they can espouse their so- called Christian philosophy of life without even mentioning the Lord Jesus Christ or His sacrificial death on the cross.

> *"These men are those who are hidden reefs in your love feasts when they feast with you without fear, caring for themselves; clouds without water, carried along by winds; autumn trees without fruit, doubly dead, uprooted;"* (Jude 12).

Plus, they do not make disciples for Christ. They are trying to get disciples to follow after themselves. Rather than preaching the gospel of the Lord Jesus Christ, they preach themselves, their families, their various ministries and how to get your money into theirpockets.

> *"For I did not shrink from declaring to you the whole purpose of God. "Be on guard for yourselves and for all the flock, among which the Holy Spirit has made you overseers, to shepherd the church of God which He purchased with His own blood. "I know that after my departure savage wolves will come in among you, not sparing the flock; and from among your own selves' men will arise, speaking perverse things, to draw away the disciples after them. "Therefore, be on the alert, remembering that night and day for a period of three years I did not cease to admonish each one*

with tears. "And now I commend you to God and to the word of His grace, which is able to build you up and to give you the inheritance among all those who are sanctified" (Acts 20:27-32 [Paul to Ephesian Elders])

So, we see the problem (false teachers) and the solution is a return to the faith which was once for all delivered to the Saints in the Holy Scriptures. Key: you have to know your Bible to determine if your teacher is true or false. That is how you compare truth with error. If you know what an actual ten-dollar bill looks and feels like you can detect any counterfeit by comparing the real with the fake.

"And He gave some as apostles, and some as prophets, and some as evangelists, and some as pastors and teachers, for the equipping of the saints for the work of service, to the building up of the body of Christ;" (Ephesians 4:11-12).

"Be reminded that all the Prophets (including the Two in Revelation, chapter 11) are for equipping the Saints for the work of service, to the building up of the Body of Christ. So, for anyone to say that the Church will not be here during their ministry (the first three and one half years), they are just simply wrong and teaching falsely. Remember the Two Prophets will be Uniting the One True Faith, but the professing (lip service) Christians will not agree with them. The departure from their teachings will result in droves leaving "the faith that was once for all delivered to the saints." Only those who start in "the Faith" and end in "the Faith" will be saved.

"Children, it is the last hour; and just as you heard that Antichrist is coming, even now many antichrists have arisen; from this we know that it is the last hour. They went out from us, but they were not really of us; for if they had been of us, they would have remained with us; but they went out, in order that it might be shown that they all are not of us. But you have an anointing from the Holy One, and you all know. I have not written to you because you do not know the truth, but because you do know it, and because no lie is of the truth" (1 John 2:18-21).

So, how long are the Saints commanded to equip the Saints for the work of service in building up the Body of Christ? Until all the Saints are spiritually mature in Christ. So, you will never finish your labor of love.

"Until we all attain to the unity of the faith, and of the knowledge of the Son of God, to a mature man, to the measure of the stature which belongs to the fullness of Christ. As a result, we are no longer to be children, tossed here and there by waves, and carried about by every wind of doctrine, by the trickery of men, by craftiness in deceitful scheming; but speaking the truth in love, we are to grow up in all aspects into Him, who is the head, even Christ," (Ephesians. 4:13-15).

So, after personal sanctification, what is the work of service? Leaders are to build up (strengthen and encourage) the other members of the Body of Christ to make the Saints strong in the Lord by having them know and understand God's word more accurately. Thus, presenting a united faith of the true Saints (The People of The Way). However, because of false teachers, many potential Saints are not getting matured. They are still children, tossed here and there by waves, and carried about by every wind of doctrine, by the trickery of men, by craftiness in deceitful scheming. We must continue speaking the truth in love, so all may grow up in all aspects into Him, who is the head, even Christ.

> *"But I say, surely Israel did not know, did they? At the first Moses says, "I will make you jealous by that which is not a nation, by a nation without understanding will I anger you"* (Romans. 10:19).

Paul said that the preaching of Moses was going to make Israel jealous and angry because God was going to give to the Gentiles what the Jews thought was exclusively theirs (the Law and their own personal God). In the same way, the preaching of the Two Prophets is to make Professing Christians jealous and angry because they do not have God's power of forgiveness. Yes, they need that power, but they will not get it until they repent from their evil and sinful practices. So, if you know you cannot stop sinning (no matter how hard you try, because you still have the sin nature), whatcan you do?

> *"I find then the principle that evil is present in me, the one who wishes to do good. For I joyfully concur with the law of God in the inner man, but*

I see a different law in the members of my body, waging war against the law of my mind, and making me a prisoner of the law of sin which is in my members. Wretched man that I am! Who will set me free from the body of this death?" (Romans 7:21-24).

When you recognize what a wretched man you are, there is hope! There are then two things you must do. What are they?

"Wretched man that I am! Who will set me free from the body of this death? Thanks be to God through Jesus Christ our Lord! So, then, on the one hand I myself with my mind am serving the law of God, but on the other, with my flesh the law of sin" (Romans 7:24-25).

First, you must believe (trust, depend on, and commit to) the Lord Jesus Christ, who is the Lamb of God who takes away the sin of the world. The second thing you must do is kill self (see Luke 9:23-27). You might say, "Isn't that an overkill?"

"And if your right eye makes you stumble, tear it out, and throw it from you; for it is better for you that one of the parts of your body perish, than for your whole body to be thrown into hell. "And if your right hand makes you stumble, cut it off, and throw it from you; for it is better for you that

one of the parts of your body perish, than for your
whole body to go into hell" (Matthew 5:29-30).

Even what Jesus said appears to be an overkill, but is it? No, He is talking about the seriousness of sin, but sinners will still find alternative ways to indulge the flesh. Again, the only way to stop sinning is to die (die to self)! Did you ever see a corpse in a funeral home? What do you remember about them? "All dressed up and no place to go?" What you should remember is the fact that in a flash (instantaneously) that person stopped sinning. The physically dead do not and cannot sin. That is why Jesus wants us to die to self- daily. Yes, we as Saints are truly alive, but we should consider ourselves as dead men who cannot sin and as such we do not sin.

> *"Therefore we have been buried with Him*
> *through baptism into death, so that as Christ*
> *was raised from the dead through the glory of the*
> *Father, so we too might walk in newness of life.*
> *For if we have become united with Him in the*
> *likeness of His death, certainly we shall be also in*
> *the likeness of His resurrection, knowing this, that*
> *our old self was crucified with Him, that our body*
> *of sin might be done away with, so that we should*
> *no longer be slaves to sin; for he who has died is*
> *freed from sin"* (Romans 6:4-7).

Remember verse seven; He who has died is free from sin, and dead men cannot sin.

"Even so consider yourselves to be dead to sin, but alive to God in Christ Jesus." (Romans 6:11).

And He was saying to them all, "If anyone wishes to come after me, let him deny himself, and take up his cross daily, and follow Me. "For whoever wishes to save his life shall lose it, but whoever loses his life for My sake, he is the one who will save it. "For what is a man profited if he gains the whole world, and loses or forfeits himself? (Luke 9:23-25).

We are to die to ourselves daily, and we are not to resurrect the dead. Have you ever asked yourself why is this apostasy (the falling away from The Scriptural Faith) going to happen? Well, surprise, it is already happening and will continue to happen even before the Antichrist comes on the scene. Why? Partly because of the Two Prophets. Those Professing Christians who are in various Christian cults will stay in those cults (and not repent), thus the Apostasy is the departing from the True Faith that was Once for All Delivered to the Saints.

If you claim to be a Christian and do not have the Holy Spirit, you will Apostatize. Thus, the preaching of the Two Prophets will help to purify the True Church and Unite the True Believers. As a result, one is more likely to have a Real Christian Soldier fighting next to him in battle, rather than the lip service ones who will go AWOL when things get tough.

"Do you suppose that I came to grant peace on earth? I tell you, no, but rather division; for from now on five members in one household will be divided, three against two, and two against three. "They will be divided, father against son, and son against father; mother against daughter, and daughter against mother; mother-in-law against daughter-in- law, and daughter-in-law against mother-in-law" (Luke 12:51-53).

Divisions happen so that the cream will rise to the top.

"For, in the first place, when you come together as a church, I hear that divisions exist among you; and in part, I believe it. For there must also be factions among you, in order that those who are approved may have become evident among you" (1 Corinthians 11:18-19).

We asked,"The Why" question about apostasy because most people in the world and even many professing Christians have never matured in the Christian faith. These professing Christians (aka, lukewarm Christians, shallow Christian, lip service Christians, baby Christians, cultural Christians, nominal Christians, and the like) are still babes even though they have been professing to be Christians for many years. They should have been teachers that give the bread of life to others, but they did not eat enough even to sustain their own lives. It will be those "old" babes who will depart because they are like the people talked about in the book of Hebrews.

"Concerning him (Melchizedek) we have much to say, and it is hard to explain, since you have become dull of hearing. For though by this time you ought to be teachers, you have need again for someone to teach you the elementary principles of the oracles of God, and you have come to need milk and not solid food. For everyone who partakes only of milk is not accustomed to the word of righteousness, for he is a babe. But solid food is for the mature, who becauseof practice have their senses trained to discern good and evil" (Hebrews 5:11-14).

So, if you want to test yourself to see if you might be one of these *lip service* Christians, write yourself a paragraph about Melchizedek. If you are unable to pass that test, then try this one! When Jesus quoted the Old Testament Scripture about, *"MAN DOES NOT LIVE BY BREAD ALONE, BUT BY EVERY WORD THAT PROCEEDS OUT OF THE MOUTH OF GOD;* What Old Testament Book was He referencing and what was the context of the quote?

Well, how did you do? Melchizedek is not the subject of many teaching pastors. So, for one to know about Melchizedek, one wouldhave to do a personal study on their own. You will have to pick up a fork and feed yourself. You must do that even if your pastor is a faithful teacher of the word.

Why is that? Because many professing Christians are spiritual anorexics. You cannot successfully live the Christian life by being bottle fed once or twice a week, and in many cases, those feeding consists of milk and cookies.

> *"Be diligent to present yourself approved to God as a workman who does not need to be ashamed, handling accurately the word of truth"* (2 Tim. 2:15).

So, what is the writer of Hebrews saying? You have to study the word of God diligently for you to grow to spiritual maturity. You will not grow to spiritual maturity if you keep depending on someone else to feed you like a baby.

> *"Do not trust in princes, in mortal man, in whom there is no salvation"* (Psalms 146:3).

You have to get off the baby bottle and pick up a fork and feed yourself. Remember, Matthew 4:4:

> *"It is written, 'MAN SHALL NOT LIVE ON BREAD ALONE, BUT ON EVERY WORD THAT PROCEEDS OUT OF THE MOUTH OF GOD.*

The answer to where this quote is found is in Deuteronomy chapter 8. So, pick up your fork (the Bible) and do not just read it, but study it, so your shallow roots may grow deep.

> *"All Scripture is inspired by God and profitable for teaching, for reproof, for correction, for training in righteousness; that the man of God*

may be adequate, equipped for every good work" (2 Timothy 3:16-17).

You will note that it does not say that the Scriptures will profit you for some good works. The Scriptures are adequate to equip you for every good work. However, the most critical work is your labor of love for your fellow man. Your study (exercising your God-given gift) is primarily for the edification of others and not for one to becomespiritually prideful.

"Knowledge makes arrogant, but love edifies" (1 Corinthians 8:1).

Thus, we are to teach the truth in love.

"But speaking the truth in love, we are to grow up in all aspects into Him, who is the head, even Christ, from whom the whole body, being fitted and held together by that which every joint supplies, accordingto the proper working of each individual part, causes the growth of the body for the building up of itself in love" (Ephesians 4:15-16).

The writer of the book, Hebrews, is writing to many Jewish listeners (Hebrews), who have to commit to what they already know is true about The Lord Jesus Christ. The key is that one must keep one's word and follow through on ones' commitments— to abide! Jesus gave us this example of a person who did not continue to endure.

"Now great multitudes were going along with Him; and He turned and said to them, "If anyone comes to Me, and does not hate his own father and mother and wife and children and brothers and sisters, yes, and even his own life, he cannot be My disciple. "Whoever does not carry his own cross and come after Me cannot be My disciple. "For which one of you, when he wants to build a tower, does not first sit down and calculate the cost, to see if he has enough to complete it? "Otherwise, when he has laid a foundation, and is not able to finish, all who observe it begin to ridicule him, saying,' this man began to build and was not able to finish'" (Luke 14:25-30).

The lack of commitment is what the writer of Hebrews is addressing. One of the reasons why these Hebrew professing Christians were not committing was due to the persecutions by their countrymen. The writer of Hebrews exhorts them to "press on" to maturity in Christ. (Hebrews 6:1).

Therefore, leaving the elementary teaching about the Christ, let us press on to maturity. Paul told Timothy to be diligent in his study and not be superficial like many who are ashamed of the gospel. True Christians are not to be ashamed of the gospel because they know it is the power of God unto salvation. The gospel message is the source of the faith that saves.

The people mentioned in the book of Hebrews have been professing Christians for a long time (Hebrews chapters 5 and

6), but they never spiritually matured. Again, you might call them *superficial Christians* or lip *service Christians*, but they are represented by the different types of soils in the parable of the sower and the seed that did not produce fruit and are not truly saved.

> *"And these are the ones who are beside the road where the word is sown; and when they hear, immediately Satan comes and takes away the word which has been sown in them. "And in a similar way these are the ones on whom seed was sown on the rocky places, who, when they hear the word,immediately receive it with joy; and they have no firm root in themselves, but are only temporary; then, when affliction or persecution arises because of the word, immediately they fall away. "And others are theones on whom seed was sown among the thorns; these are the ones who have heard the word, and theworries of the world, and the deceitfulness of riches, and the desires for other things enter in and chokethe word, and it becomes unfruitful"* (Mark 4:15-19).

These superficial Christians are so immature that they do not even understand the elementary principles of Law or Faith. They might have faith in God, but they do not have the faith that saves. These babes do not know or understand God's laws or why God gave them to us in the first place? One needs to know and understand law to accurately determine what is right and what is wrong behavior. These babies fail to do that, and like babies, they cannot do or even understand godly behavior of living righteously before God and men.

"For everyone who partakes only of milk is not accustomed to the word of righteousness, for he is a babe" (Hebrews 5:13).

Ligonier's Ministries and Lifeway Research take a "State of Theology" survey every two years. Their most recent polling of religious Americans states that "Americans in general and evenevangelicals are "slipping." Half of the evangelicals, for example, think God accepts the worship of all religions." Wow! When you believe that God accepts the worship of all religions, you are admitting you do not know the difference between right and wrong, good and evil, and even God and the Devil.

The reason they cannot tell the difference between God and the Devil is simply that for many of them their god is the Devil. (John 8:43-47). By espousing such a belief, one is stating that Jesus is not the only way to the Father as He claimed (John 14:6).

"Jesus said to him, "I am the way, and the truth, and the life; no one comes to the Father, but through Me" (John 14:6).

This group in the survey are also stating that there is no one truth as to how God wants to be worshiped. God tells us how He wants to be worshiped. He wants to be worshiped in spirit and truth and in no other way. God is a Spirit, and His Word is The Truth.

You are His creation, and it is His ball (planet Earth), and He determines how He wants to be worshiped. You cannot be a liberal like Cain, who thought he could worship God, "his *way.*"

> *"And the Lord had regard for Abel and for his offering; but for Cain and for his offering he had no regard. So Cain became very angry and his countenance fell. Then the Lord said to Cain, "Why are you angry? And why has your countenance fallen? "If you do well, will not your countenance be lifted up? And if you do not do well, sin is crouching at the door; and its desire is for you, but you must master it." And Cain told Abel his brother. And it came about when they were in the field, that Cain (rose up against Abel his brother and killed him"* (Genesis 4:4-8).

What do we see here? Cain killed his brother Abel because God told Cain he was wrong in his worship and he had to repent of his wrongdoing. However, Cain's response was to kill his righteous brother (Abel) who worshiped God the right way. The unrighteouswill kill the righteous when one tells them they are doing wrong, and that their deeds are evil and sinful in God's sight.

> *"For this is the message which you have heard from the beginning, that we should love one*

another; not as Cain, who was of the evil one, and slew his brother. And for what reason did he slay him? Because his deeds were evil, and his brothers were righteous" (1 John 3:11-12).

The evil people (like Cain) will kill the righteous because they, get frustrated and angry and respond with physical violence. Jesus told the woman at the well and all of us who read the Scriptures as to how God wants to be worshiped.

"Jesus said to her, "Woman, believe Me, an hour is coming when neither in this mountain, nor in Jerusalem, shall you worship the Father. "You worship that which you do not know; we worship that which we know, for salvation is from the Jews. "But an hour is coming, and now is, when the true worshipers shall worship the Father in spirit and truth; for such people the Father seeks to be His worshipers. "God is spirit, and those who worship Him must worship in spirit and truth" (John 4:21-25)

Evangelicals today do not take this Scripture and many other Scriptures to heart. They think the way you worship God is through music. They have what is called by many *7-11 choruses*, seven words, repeated 11 times. Their fast-upbeat songs are their praise songs, and their slower beat songs are their worship songs. The truth is that music has become their primary way of worship rather than having the word of God taught and explained to them. This principle is born out in that they stand for the singing and sit for the Scripture readings.

They used to call the Roman Mass the "The Poor Man's Opera." The rich went to the opera, and the poor went to the other entertainment center. However, the same idea is happening in our churches today. You give your money; you get entertained by the show, the music, the plays, the skits, the processions, and the like. You then get permission to do crazy antics in public and then you get rewarded with a worthless fire insurance policy just for attending the show.

The people of God must understand that Christianity is not a "Spectator Sport." You are the players, and you are actively playing on the field of battle. The only spectators are the non-believers. (Matthew 5:16). Paul put it this way:

> *"Do you not know that those who run in a race all run, but only one receives the prize? Run in such a way that you may win,…." (1 Corinthians 9:24)*

You are not competing against other Christians (in the race), you have to run your race, and you must run to win even if no one (except God) is watching you. You must be men and women of integrity.

> *"Do you not know that those who run in a race, all run, but only one receives the prize? Run in such a way that you may win. Everyone who competes in the games exercises self-control in all things. they*

then do it to receive a perishable wreath, but we an imperishable. (To be a winner you cannot be a couch potato, you must discipline your mind and body and have self-control in all things. Athletes do what they do to receive a medal, trophy or wreath, but the people of God run the race to receive an imperishable crown). *Therefore I run in such a way, as not without aim; I box in such a way, as not beating the air; but I buffet my body and make it my slave, lest possibly, after I have preached to others, I myself should be disqualified"* (1 Corinthians. 9:24- 27).

Paul was a winner and victor! His goal was to be victorious. He did not just go through the motions of being a runner or boxer. He exercised self-discipline and conditioned himself and made sure he played according to the rules so that he would not be disqualified. Paul was a participant in the action and did not go to the church/synagogue buildings to be entertained. Many professing Christians today do not understand that the church buildings should be their Bible teaching schools and not their entertainment centers.

The survey, as mentioned above, further stated that "fifty-five percent of evangelicals believe that while everyone sins a little, most people are good by nature." With that mindset, you do not need a savior, and it's probably one of their many reasons for not evangelizing.

"What then? Are we better than they? Not at all; for we have already charged that both Jews and Greeks are all under sin;" (Romans 3:9).

That is the universal charge by God against all of humanity.

"As it is written, "THERE IS NONE RIGHTEOUS, NOT EVEN ONE; THERE IS NONE WHO UNDERSTANDS, THERE IS NONE WHO SEEKS FOR GOD; ALL HAVE TURNED ASIDE, TOGETHER THEY HAVE BECOME USELESS; THERE IS NONE WHO DOES GOOD, THERE IS NOT EVEN ONE." "THEIR THROAT IS AN OPEN GRAVE, WITH THEIR TONGUES THEY KEEP DECEIVING," "THE POISON OF ASPS IS UNDER THEIR LIPS"; "WHOSE MOUTH IS FULL OF CURSING AND BITTERNESS"; "THEIR FEET ARE SWIFT TO SHED BLOOD, DESTRUCTION AND MISERY ARE IN THEIR PATHS, AND THE PATH OF PEACE HAVE THEY NOT KNOWN. "THERE IS NO FEAR OF GOD BEFORE THEIR EYES." Now we know that whatever the Law says, it speaks to those who are under the Law, that every mouth may be closed, and all the world may become accountable to God; because by the works of the Law no flesh will be justified in his sight; for through the Law comes the knowledge of sin" (Rom.3:10-20).

Remember where God had Moses put the Ten Commandments that were given him and the people; next to the ark of the covenant, but why? As a testimony or witness against them. It was not to tell them how good they were it was to tell them how bad they were.

> "And it came about, when Moses finished writing the words of this law in a book until they were complete, that Moses commanded the Levites who carried the ark of the covenant of the LORD, saying, "Take this book of the law and place it beside the ark of the covenant of the LORD your God, that it may remain there as a witness against you. For I know your rebellion and your stubbornness; behold, while I am still alive with you today, you have beenrebellious against the LORD; how much more, then, after my death? "Assemble to me all the elders of your tribes and your officers, that I may speak these words in their hearing and call the heavens and the earth to witness against them" (Deuteronomy 31:24- 28).

The Law was a witness against them. The reason that many people are lost is that they do not understand the Law or even understand that they are under the Law. Through the Law comesthe knowledge of sin, but if you do not know that all people are sinners, it proves you do not know the Law. Those in the study would also be saying something like this, "I know I sin a little, but overall, I am a good person."

However, they fail to remember what Jesus said, "There is no one good but God" (Luke 18:19).

Yes, many will depart from the once for all delivered faith, because they do not have their senses trained in living righteously. They will compromise what little faith they have and will not resist sin because they do not hate sin as God hates it. They love themselves; their sinful ways and they do not want to change. Whereas the mature Christian knows he "was" a sinner, but now he is a Saint (a Holy One separated from sin). He instinctively knows the difference between good and evil and right and wrong, and lives by the faith given to him by God and knows the truth when he hears it. He is not a hypocrite because he acts upon what he knows to be true. He understands the Spirit of the Law as well as the Letter of the Law. But the reality is that, "They are a law to themselves".... (Romans 2:14-16). He instinctively knows what is right and what is wrong behavior. What has just been said is extremely important about the Spirit of the Law. The Spirit of the Law is instinctive because it is Written on the Hearts of the People of The Way. It is our internal witness, which is the combination of the Holy Spirit's Presence and the individual's conscience.

> *"For when Gentiles who do not have the Law* (the Letter of the Law) *do instinctively the things of the Law* (the Spirit of the Law), *these, not having the Law* (Letter), *are a law to themselves* (internally), *in that they show the work of the Law written in their hearts, their conscience bearing*

witness, and their thoughts alternately accusing or else defending them, on the day when, according to my gospel, God will judge the secrets of men through Christ Jesus" (Rom. 2:14-16).

So, who are the saved ones who will endure to the end? Those who have been truly born again from above and are mature having the mind of Christ and the Spirit of the Law written on their hearts. They understand the mind of God, and they comprehend what God is doing and why He does what He does? They have overcome the evil one, and they read and apply God's word in their lives.

"I am writing to you, little children, because your sins are forgiven you for His name's sake. I am writing to you, fathers, because you know Him who has been from the beginning. I am writing to you, young men, because you have overcome the evil one. I have written to you, children, because you know the Father. I have written to you, fathers, because you know Him who has been from the beginning. I have written to you, young men, because you are strong, and the word of God abides in you, and you have overcome the evil one" (1 John 2:12- 14).

You will note that "babes" are not mentioned by John. One has to grow out of the baby state quickly (like the animals in the wild who have to get running with the heard – asap). The little children at least know their sins are forgiven for His name's sake. However, even the little children must grow up to become young men because young men are strong in the word (unlike little children) and the young men have also overcome the evil one. The little children have a child-like faith that needs strengthening as well; they have not as yet overcome the schemes of the Devil.

> *"Therefore leaving the elementary teaching about the Christ, let us press on to maturity,... and this we shall do, if God permits"* (Hebrews 6:1-3).

Why must these little children press on to maturity? Because they are still not strong in the word (faith) and they have not overcome the evil schemes of the Devil. Jesus prayed to the Father to protect them from the evil one, but that comes with the individual having a strong abiding faith in God.

> *"Be of sober spirit, be on the alert. Your adversary, the devil, prowls about like a roaring lion, seeking someone to devour. But resist him, firm in your faith, knowing that the same experiences of suffering are being accomplished by your brethren who are in the world"* (1 Peter 5:8-9 warning to the little children).

Babes cannot and do not resist because they do not have a faith that saves and secures them. The more mature Christians, the *young men,* and the *fathers* are strong, and the word of God abides in them. They also know and have overcome the schemes of the evil one. So, God's exhortation to His children is to *grow up* and be strong and courageous in the faith that was given to them from the Scriptures. One becomes strong in the faith when one knows and understand the Scriptures.

> *"So faith comes from hearing, and hearing by the word of Christ" (Romans 10:17).*

> *"And He gave some as apostles, and some as prophets, and some as evangelists, and some as pastors and teachers, for the equipping of the saints for the work of service, to the building up of the body of Christ; until we all attain to the unity of the faith, and of the knowledge of the son of God, to a mature man, to the measure of the stature which belongs to the fulness of Christ. As a result, we are no longer to be children, tossed here and there by waves, and carried about by every wind of doctrine, by the trickery of men, by craftiness in deceitful scheming; but speaking the truth in love, we are to grow up in allaspects into Him, who is the head, even Christ," (Ephesians 4:11-15).*

God's children have to grow up in all aspects into Him, because if they do not grow up and become mature in the faith, theywill depart from the faith when the persecution comes upon them.

#6 THE PROPHETIC WITNESSES

There are six Significant Witnesses or Prophets that God specifically wants us to listen too. Who are they? Moses, Elijah, the Lord Jesus Christ, John the Baptist, and the Two Witnesses in Revelation chapter 11. At this point we are assigning names to the Two Witnesses in Revelation 11. We will be calling the Prophet like Moses and like the Lord Jesus Christ—"**JAMES**" (**J**esus **A**nd **M**oses **E**xtol **S**alvation) and the Prophet like Elijah and John the Baptist— "**U R2 JOHN**" (**Y**ou **A**re **T**o **J**oin **O**ur **H**oly **N**ation).

What do all six of these Witnesses have in common? Well, they are representatives of all the Scriptural Teachings of the Law and the Prophets. God wants you to listen to all His Prophets, but these six in particular. If you do not listen and obey all of God's prophets, you will come under the Judgment of God. You must believe God and that belief is in what the Witnesses/Prophets said, did, and wrote. The Faith that saves is not your Faith. It is His Faith (His Word that becomes your Faith) that is given to you as a Gift of God.

"For by grace you have been saved through faith; and that not of yourselves, it is the gift of God; not

as a result of works, that no one should boast. For
we are His workmanship, created in Christ Jesus
for good works, which God prepared beforehand,
that we should walk in them" (Ephesians 2:8-10).

That is why you have to defend the faith that was once
for all delivered to the Saints (Jude 3,4), because your faith is
the faith given to you as a gift from God, and that is why you
must accurately present His faith to the world. So, if someone
asks you about your faith, you will tell them that your faith
is the faith given to you by God, and that is what Jesus said
and believed!

"Jesus therefore answered them, and said, "My
teaching is not mine, but His who sent Me. "If any
man is willing to do His will, he shall know of the
teaching, whether it is of God, or whether I
speak from Myself. "He who speaks from himself
seeks his own glory; but He who is seeking the glory
of the one who sent Him, He is true, and there is
no unrighteousness in Him" (John 7:16-18).

The Biblical meaning of believing is to trust, depend
on, rely on, and commit to the teaching of the written Word
which tells us about the Living Word of God which is
The Lord Jesus Christ. You must understand that having
a personal opinion about a Jesus is not salvation. Everyone
believes in a Jesus, even if their own Jesus is the Devil or even
a figment of their own imagination. However, to have saving
faith, you must believe in the Jesus of the Scriptures. If you

do not believe in the Jesus of the Bible, your faith is in vain (worthless and without value).

> *"Now I make known to you, brethren, the gospel which I preached to you, which also you received, in which also you stand, by which also you are saved, if you hold fast the word which I preached to you, unless you believed in vain"* (1 Corinthians 15:1-2).

Yes, the Two Prophets in the Book of the Revelation are not on the scene yet, but again, they will only illumine and carry out what the other Prophets have already spoken or written.

So, in the meantime, you would do well to listen to all the Witnesses/Prophets that have already come and witnessed in the Scriptures. Wake Up, Listen Up, or Go Down!

Jesus sacrificed Himself for the good of others, and God expects us (the people of The Way) to sacrifice ourselves for the good of others as well. Jesus Christ is our example and His command to us is that we love as He loved.

> *""A new commandment I give to you, that you love one another, even as I have loved you, that you also love one another. "By this all men will know that you are My disciples, if you have love for one another"* (John 13:34-35).

"We know love by this, that He laid down His life for us; and we ought to lay down our lives for the brethren" (1 John 3:16).

We love because He first loved us.

"We love, because He first loved us. If someone says, "I love God," and hates his brother, he is a liar; for the one who does not love his brother whom he has seen, cannot love God whom he has not seen. And this commandment we have from Him, that the one who loves God should love his brother also" (1 John 4:19-21).

Jesus said you would know the true people of God (His disciples) by their love. If you do not produce acts of love - (to people – to produce fruit), you are not a true disciple no matter what you say. You will be known by what you do and not only by what yousay; because talk is cheap. Jesus said that most religious people worship God with their lips (lip service people), but their hearts are far from Him (see Mark 7:6-7).

"A new commandment I give to you, that you love one another, even as I have loved you, that you also love one another. "By this all men will know that you are My disciples, if you have love for one another" (John 13:34-35).

The opposite of love is not hate. The opposite of love is selfishness. Selfish people are not loving, so it is only selfless people who will endure to the end. Genuinely loving people will love God and others, even more than they love themselves.

> *"Now the salvation, and the power, and the kingdom of our God and the authority of His Christ have come, for the accuser of our brethren has been thrown down, who accuses them before our God day and night. "And they overcame him because of the blood of the lamb and because of the word of their testimony, and they did not love their life even to death"* (Revelations 12:10-11).

If you are selfish and think only about yourself, you will have all eternity to do that, but if you love God and others, you will have all eternity to do that, too.

> *"For whoever wishes to save his life shall lose it; but whoever loses his life for my sake and the gospel's shall save it. "For what does it profit a man to gain the whole world, and forfeit his soul? "For what shall a man give in exchange for his soul? "For whoever is ashamed of Me and My words in this adulterous and sinful generation, the Son of Man will also be ashamed of him when He comes in the glory of His Father with the holy angels"* (Mark 8:35-38).

A true Christian cannot love the world and the things in the world (including their own lives); because if you do love the world and the things in the world, then that means you do not have a love of the Father in you, and you are not truly saved.

> *"Now great multitudes were going along with Him; and He turned and said to them, "If anyone comes to Me, and does not hate his own Father and mother and wife and children and brothers and sisters, yes, and even his own life, he cannot be My disciple. "Whoever does not carry his own cross and come after Me cannot be My disciple"* (Luke 14:25-27).

The things that most people love in the world are the loves that God hates.

> *"Do not love the world, nor the things in the world. If anyone loves the world, the love of the Father isnot in him. For all that is in the world, the lust of the flesh and the lust of the eyes and the boastful prideof life, is not from the Father, but is from the world. And the world is passing away, and also its lusts; but the one who does the will of God abides forever"* (1 John 2:15-17).

Jesus said that there was no one greater than John the Baptist. Why? Because he was God's man doing God's will in the right place and at the right time.

> *""Truly, I say to you, among those born of women there has not arisen anyone greater than*

John the Baptist; yet he who is least in the kingdom
of heaven is greater than he" (Matthew 11:11)

You, as a believer, are more significant than John the Baptist? If you are a Saint (having the resurrected Spirit of Christ in you), then you are more significant even than the great John the Baptist. Even if you think you got into the kingdom by the skin of your teeth, you are still superior to John the Baptist.

Why should this statement by Jesus be encouraging to the present-day Saints? Because everyone who has the gift of the Spirit of Christ dwelling in them is greater than the greatest Old Testament Prophet. The Book of Hebrews chapter 11 writes about the men and women of faith. What was the footnote for those saints?

"Men of whom the world was not worthy)"
(Hebrews 11:38).

The same is true for all the New Testament Saints, in that, the world is not worthy to even have you with them.

""If the world hates you, you know that it has
hated Me before it hated you. "If you were of the
world, the world would love its own; but because
you are not of the world, but I chose you out of
the world, therefore the world hates you" (John
15:18-19).

Men should seek God their Creator and ask God, what do you require of me, or what do you want from me? God tells us in simple terms what He wants. To do His will and His will is that none should perish but all come to repentance (2 Peter 3:9).

> *"He has told you, O man, what is good; and what does the Lord require of you but to do justice, to love kindness, and to walk humbly with your God?"* (Micah. 6:8).

The problem is that the majority of people do not do these things. Yes, man knows what is good and right, but they do not practice the good that they know.

> *"Therefore, to one who knows the right thing to do, and does not do it, to him it is sin"* (James 4:17).

A man knows there is a God because of God's creation. Men may not know who that creator is, but they instinctively know that there is a Creator God. If they say otherwise, they are liars.

> *"The heavens are telling of the glory of God; and their expanse is declaring the work of His hands. Day to day pours forth speech, and night to night reveals knowledge. There is no speech, nor are there words; their voice is not heard"* (Psalm 19:1-3).

God is speaking through His creation, are you listening? Thus, one of God's most excellent witnesses for His existence is His creation. Another way that man knows there is a God is by man's conscience. When he does wrong; why does he feel guilty? It is because God gave him a conscience. Thus, God tells us that He is known by His creation and by the conscience that He has given to man.

God gives man both external and internal witnesses, so all of humanity is without excuse about there being a God. That is why hell's judgments are so severe. It is because men are not ignorant, they know what is right and good, but they are rebellious and will notdo what they know is right.

> *"For the wrath of God is revealed from heaven against all ungodliness and unrighteousness of men, who suppress the truth in unrighteousness, because that which is known about God is evident within them; for God made it evident to them. For since the creation of the world His invisible attributes, His eternal power and divine nature, have been clearly seen, being understood through what has been made, so that they are without excuse. For eventhough they knew God, they did not honor Him as God, or give thanks; but they became futile in their speculations, and their foolish heart was darkened. Professing to be wise, they became fools, and exchanged the glory of the incorruptible God for an image in the form of corruptible man and of birds and four-footed animals and crawling creatures"* (Romans 1:18-23).

Then God gave to man a third witness --- The Holy Scriptures. You know there is a God by His creation and by your conscience, but again you still may not know who that God is. So, God gives you the third witness of the Scriptures that tells you who that God is that created you and why?

"I will give thanks to Thee, for I am fearfully and wonderfully made; wonderful are Thy works, and my soul knows it very well" (Psalms 139:14)

Then when you truly believe the Scriptures from the heart, God gives you another internal witness of His Holy Spirit. So, there are two external witnesses. (creation and the Scriptures), and two internal witnesses (your conscience and His Holy Spirit).

Also, God uses the Scriptures to sharpen man's conscience, so he can even more accurately know right from wrong and good from evil. The witnesses mentioned above are sufficient to get man's attention to believe in God and repent of their evil deeds. So, why will men still not believe and repent? Because they suppress what they instinctively know to be true. They deceive themselves. They are not seeking God, nor are they seeking the truth, and they end up believing what is false. God is seeking, but because of sin, men are hiding. Remember Adam and Eve? What did they do after they sinned? They hid!

"And they heard the sound of the Lord God walking in the garden in the cool of the day, and the man and his wife hid themselves from the presence of the Lord God among the trees of the garden. Then the Lord God called to the man,

and said to him, "Where are you?" And he said, "I heard the sound of Thee in the garden, and I was afraid because I was naked; so I hid myself." And He said, "Who told you that you were naked?" (Gen.3:8-11).

God asks Adam, "Who told you that you were naked? He did not answer, but he knew it instinctively. His conscience told him he was naked and guilty and thus his reason for hiding.

"And this is the judgment, that the light is come into the world, and men loved the darkness rather than the light; for their deeds were evil. "For everyone who does evil hates the light, and does not come to the light, lest his deeds should be exposed. "But he who practices the truth comes to the light, that his deeds may be manifested as having been wrought in God" (John 3:19-21).

The truth is that men do not see because they do not want to see. Yes, they are blinded by God, the Devil, the Sin Nature and by their own willful blindness. But if they seek the miracle of salvation through The Lord Jesus Christ, their spiritual eyes can be opened.

"And even if our gospel is veiled, it is veiled to those who are perishing, in whose case the god of this world has blinded the minds of the unbelieving, that they might not see the light of

the gospel of the glory of Christ, who is the image
of God"(2 Cor.4:3-4)

They do not know God because they do not want to know God. They are like thieves looking out for the policemen. The thieves are not looking for the policeman; they are looking out for the policeman. The following verses contain great promises to all those who are genuinely seeking God.

> *""If **any man** is willing to do His will, he*
> *shall know of the teaching, whether it is of God, or*
> *whether I speak from myself. "He who speaks from*
> *himself seeks his own glory; but He who is seeking*
> *the glory of the one who sent Him, He is true, and*
> *there is no unrighteousness in Him"* (John 7:17-18
> Jesus speaking)

If anyone or whoever is willing to do the will of God, they will know if the teachings are from God and true or whether the teachings are not from God and false. God also has a few other ways of getting man's attention to repent (other than creation, conscience, the Holy Spirit and the Bible), but men do not like God's alternative ways either. They do not seek God, nor do they want to hear from God. Their thinking is like this, "I will leave God alone if He leaves me alone." However, they better be careful about what they wish because God may answer their rejection of Himself by His rejection of them.

> *"It is for discipline that you endure; God*
> *deals with you as with sons; for what son is there*

whom his father does not discipline? But if you are without discipline, of which all have become partakers, then you are illegitimate children and not sons" (Hebrews 12:7-8)

Their request of being left alone better not happen, because God wants all men to come to repentance and He does not want anyone to perish.

""Say to them, 'As I live!' declares the Lord God, 'I take no pleasure in the death of the wicked, but rather that the wicked turn from his way and live. Turn back, turn back from your evil ways! Why then will you die, O house of Israel?" (Ezekiel 33:11).

Some of the other ways that God tries to get man's attention is through sickness, pain and suffering, drought, famine, pestilence, taking away one's wealth, natural catastrophes that happen to them and to others. Thus, these are some of the attention-getting signs that the two Revelation Prophets will give.

"If a trumpet is blown in a city will not the people tremble? If a calamity occurs in a city has not the Lord done it?" (Amos 3:6).

When you hear about or experience any of God's attention-getting signs than what is your response? Hopefully, it would be best if you realized your human frailty and that you are still on Earth living in a fallen (Humpty Dumpty) world.

Plus, this world is filled with the corrupt world systems that are controlled by the evil one. And because of the fall of man (in Adam), everyone and everything has fallen and is broken, including nature.

Take special note that nature is not friendly, and you should learn that from natural disasters. No matter where you live, you are subject to nature's fury and thus the blowing of God's trumpet. The blowing of the trumpet (the shofar) was a call to assemble and also a call to war. Have you made peace with God, yet?

> *"Now therefore, O kings, show discernment; take warning, O judges of the earth. Worship the LORD with reverence and rejoice with trembling. Do homage to the Son, lest He become angry, and you perish in the way, for His wrath may soon be kindled. How blessed are all who take refuge in Him"* (Psalms 2:10-12).

Not only is nature fallen, but then there are the fallen demonic systems, like all government systems, religious systems, economic systems, political systems, social systems, educational systems, entertainment systems and the like. These are the corrupt, perverted systems in the world that the people idolize but God hates because they are filled with the world's lies, stumbling blocks, and deceptions.

> *""Woe to the world because of its stumbling blocks! For it is inevitable that stumbling blocks*

come; but woe to that man through whom the stumbling block comes!" (Matthew 18:7).

"I have not written to you because you do not know the truth, but because you do know it, and because no lie is of the truth" (1 John 2:21).

E. g., If you hear about a tornado doing destruction and killing people or hear about many people getting killed by a crazed mass shooter, how do you respond to such events? Think about it! That is often the problem? People do not think much about it, and whenthey do think about it they come to the wrong conclusions. They want to ban guns and make more laws, but what good are laws ifthe people are lawless. People do not take the death or the loss of one's soul seriously. Do you blame God, guns or even the victims for being stupid and careless, or do you take it to heart and realize how fragile all life is including your own? God's solution is that you repent and stop your rebellion against God and your fellow man!

"If trumpet is blown in a city will not the people tremble? If a calamity occurs in a city has not the Lord done it? Surely the Lord God does nothing unless He reveals His secret counsel to His servants the prophets. A lion has roared! Who will not fear? The Lord God has spoken! Who can but prophesy?" (Amos 3:6-8).

Catastrophic events are all permitted by God. Why? Because if God judged sin immediately when it happened than non of us would have made it to our first birthday. He is blowing a trumpet, and people should hear of these devastating events and fear. He then tells His Prophets to roar and proclaim what He has permitted and what He is planning to do in the future. So, what we should learn from all these various catastrophic events, is that we must be consistently prepared to meet Our Maker, because you will not always get an advanced warning.

You have probably heard the trumpet blow many times throughout your life, but have you listened, and are you ready to war with God, or are you at peace with Him? It would be best if you are prepared for action. Remember: Your life could come to an abrupt end without any further trumpet warnings. So, you must be a good Boy Scout and always be prepared to meet your Maker.

> *"Therefore, just as the Holy Spirit says,"Today if you hear His voice, do not harden your hearts as when they provoked Me, as in the day of trial in the wilderness,"* (Hebrews 3:7-8).

Do not let the day you die be the most significant negative surprise of your life?

> *"For, "ALL FLESH IS LIKE GRASS, AND ALL ITS GLORY LIKE THE FLOWER OF GRASS. THE GRASS WITHERS, AND THE FLOWER FALLS OFF, BUT THE WORD OF THE LORD ABIDES FOREVER." And this*

is the word which was preached to you (1 Peter 1:24-25).

Jesus tells us what one's response should be after describing two catastrophes. One a man-made catastrophe and the other a natural catastrophe.

> *"Now on the same occasion there were some present who reported to Him about the Galileans, whose blood Pilate had mingled with their sacrifices. and He answered and said to them, "Do you suppose that these Galileans were greater sinners than all other Galileans, because they suffered this fate? "I tell you, no, but unless you repent, you will all likewise perish. "Or do you suppose that those eighteen on whom the tower in psyllium fell and killed them, were worse culprits than all the men who live in Jerusalem? "I tell you, no, but unless you repent, you will all likewise perish"* (Luke 13:1-5).

So, how did Jesus say one should respond to these two catastrophes? By repenting! God is going to use various tools in His arsenal to get people to repent. God does not want men to continue in their rebellion against Him by following the rebellious deeds of the Devil. If you do not Wake Up, Listen Up, you will Go Down with the Devil.

> *""Say to them, 'As I live!' declares the Lord God, 'I take no pleasure in the death of the wicked, but rather that the wicked turn from his way*

and live. Turn back, turn back from your evil ways! Why then will you die, O house of Israel?" (Ezekiel. 33:11).

Jesus and John the Baptist constantly preached, "Repent, for the Kingdom of Heaven is at hand."

"From that time Jesus began to preach and say, "Repent, for the kingdom of heaven is at hand" (Matthew 4:17).

The Father also tried to get man's attention by sending His Son (Mark 12:1-12). King Jesus was ministering on Earth for over three years, and He was showing the people what the King and His Kingdom were like. He fed them, healed the sick, raised the dead and even showed them that He had control over nature (like walking on water and calming the storm). However, many of the Jewish leaders wrongly interpreted His message, and they influenced the people to reject the King and His Kingdom.

"They therefore cried out, "Away with Him, away with Him, crucify Him!" Pilate said to them, "Shall I crucify your King?" The chief priests answered, "We have no king but Caesar." So he then delivered Him to them to be crucified" (John 19:15-16).

So, people do not like God's solutions to their unbelief. Why? Because they are content in their unbelief and sinful ways, whereas God is not. All men must repent or come under the judgment of God. Unrepentant sinners cannot enter the Kingdom of God.

> *"And Jesus, looking around, said to his disciples, "How hard it will be for those who are wealthy to enter the kingdom of God!" And the disciples were amazed at his words. but Jesus answered again and said to them, "Children, how hard it is to enter the kingdom of God! 'It is easier for a camel to go through the eye of a needle than for a rich man to enter the kingdom of God." And they were even more astonished and said to Him, "Then who can be saved?" Looking upon them, Jesus said, "With men it is impossible, but not with God; for all things are possible with God"* (Mark 10:23-27).

As you know, Jesus said it is impossible for men to save themselves, and it is impossible for those who are rich to get to heaven. Why? Because they trust in themselves and their riches rather than trusting in God. They do not want God nor do they see a need for Him. They don't thank God for their daily bread because they feel that they worked for it and they earned their money. They fail to realize that their ability to work and to accumulate wealth is a gift of God. Everything that man possesses including his physical skills and abilities are a gift from God.

> *"Furthermore, as for every man to whom God has given riches and wealth, he has also empowered him to eat from them and to receive his reward*

and rejoice in his labor; this is the gift of God"
(Ecclesiastes 5:19).

God knows that men will only come around to accept Him and thank Him when their means of getting bread (food) are gone. Thus, explaining the need for hard times during the Tribulation. Then, men will again pray to God, "Give us this day our daily bread." God knows men's hearts, and He is seeking those who are willing to do His will.

> *""But an hour is coming, and now is, when the trueworshipers shall worship the Father in spirit and truth; for such people the Father seeks to be his worshipers. "God is spirit, and those who worship Him must worship in spirit and truth." The woman said to Him, "I know that Messiah is coming (He who is called Christ); when that one comes, He will declare all things to us." Jesus said to her, "I who speak to you am He"* (John 4:23-26 Jesus speaking).

#7 THE CASE AGAINST DISPENSATIONALISM

End time predictive prophecy teachings for the people of The Way is like a puzzle. It is not a puzzle, but it is "like" a puzzle.

> *"It is the glory of God to conceal a matter,* but the glory of kings is *to search out a matter"* (Proverbs 25:2).

However, to the natural man, it is a puzzle and puzzling. They cannot get the puzzle pieces to fit, so they throw some away (like the Law pieces) and force pieces in places where they do not fit. The simplest and most important part of a puzzle is the outer frame. Pieces that are straight on the sides and the corner pieces are apparent, but one must put the frame together first to understand the big picture. The proper outer frame is essential. Many may have set many parts and sections together correctly in the middle, but if your outer frame is not correct, the puzzle's picture will never be understood or completed.

The frames of many prophecy teachers are incredibly flawed, and that prevents them from understanding what God is presently doing and what He will do in the future.

They are deceived and thus deceiving. Most importantly, they are not maturing the Saints and preparing The People of The Way for the tough times that lie ahead.

> *"But when He, the Spirit of truth, comes, He will guide you into all the truth; for He will not speak on His own initiative, but whatever He hears, He will speak; and He will disclose to you what is to come"* (John 16:13).

The Spirit of Truth will not guide you in some truth; He will guide you into all the truth, which includes end-time events (events that are to come). The Father will instruct the Spirit, and the Spirit will teach us. The reason that there are so many different teachings under the Christendom umbrella is due to the simple fact that many of these teachers are void of the Spirit. If the Spirit is to guide you into all truth and you teach error, then you become suspect of being a natural man trying to understand a spiritual book.

> *"But a natural man does not accept the things of the Spirit of God; for they are foolishness to him, and he cannot understand them, because they are spiritually appraised. But he who is spiritual appraises all things, yet he himself is appraised by no man. For "WHO HAS KNOWN THE MIND OF THE LORD, THAT HE SHOULD INSTRUCT HIM? But we have the mind of Christ"* (1 Corinthians 2:14-16).

First and foremost, you must believe in the literal interpretation of the Scriptures. However, that being said, you must also accurately divide the Word of Truth.

> *"Be diligent to present yourself approved to God as a workman who does not need to be ashamed, handling accurately the word of truth"* (2 Timothy 2:15).

> *"Surely the Lord God does nothing unless He reveals His secret counsel to His servants the prophets. A lion has roared! Who will not fear? The Lord God has spoken! Who can but prophesy?"* (Amos 3:7-8).

The picture frame of the Christian Dispensationalist is very flawed. According to Dispensationalist Teachings, "The Day of the Lord" starts from the Pretribulation Rapture and ends at the end of the Tribulation Period and sometimes even longer. As such, it is difficult for them to know where to put the puzzle pieces of future events. Their most significant error is in the area that they pride themselves the most, that is in the area of Grace. They call the "Church Age, The Age of Grace," but they overlook the fact that no one was ever justified either in the New or Old Testaments without Grace and Faith. Some of these teachers even go so far as to say that an individual was Justified (Saved) by keeping the Law in the Old Testament and by Grace in the New. This is simply false teaching. No one was ever Justified (Saved), by doing the works of the Law, (unless one considers the Sacrificial System as part of the Law), but again that is a demonstration of God's Grace and Faith).

> *"For by grace you have been saved through faith; and that not of yourselves, it is the gift of God; not as a result of works, that no one should boast"* (Ephesians 2:8-9).

Again, be reminded that the judgment of God begins with the household of God. These Two Revelation Prophets will start the countdown to the Rapture, The Day of the LORD, Armageddon and the Lord's Second Coming. That having been said, "The Book of theRevelation" is the revelation (the revealing) of the Lord Jesus Christ (The Faithful Witness) and not the revelation of the Devil (Rev. 1:5).

The opening of the seven seals scroll by The Lord Jesus Christ is God's blueprint for His Christ's rise and Satan's demise. It tells us how God will destroy the kings and the kingdoms of this world and replace them with the Kingdom of His beloved Son.

> *"And in the days of those kings the God of heaven will set up a kingdom which will never be destroyed, and that kingdom will not be left for another people; it will crush and put an end to all these kingdoms, but it will itself endure forever"* (Daniel 2:44).

This book will be critical of the Christian Dispensational teachings about end times. Why? Because judgment begins at the household of God and they are teaching falsely.

"Those whom I love, I reprove and discipline; be zealous therefore, and repent" (Revelation 3:19).

Most professing Christians who are Dispensationalist might not even know that they are one of them. So, you do not have to worry about understanding that teaching to understand what is being written here. One thing that you should know about the Dispensationalist Teachings is that it has nothing to do with how one is saved. It has to do with men trying to systematize the Scriptures, and in the process, they have created many faulty presuppositions. These faulty presuppositions end up becoming traditional teachings by men that other men blindly follow to their detriment and even destruction. Is that serious? Yes! Because truth and error is error (Mark 7:6-12), and no lie is of the truth.

You cannot approach the Scriptures with preconceived ideas or Presuppositional Teachings. You must exegete the Scriptures correctly, that is to "take out the explanation" of what is said and not put in what you would like it to say. Dispensationalist do not let the Scriptures speak for themselves. For them, the Scriptures have to go through the grid of the Dispensational Periods, and as such, they are forced to believe in a Pretribulation Rapture. Again, "Dispensationalism has nothing to do with Salvation." However, when it comes to their so-called "Church Age" or "Age of Grace," they lose it.

Their "Age of Grace" or their "Church Age," forces them into a Pretribulation Rapture Theory.

Thus, they create a faulty start of "The Day of the LORD." Some people are saved in this Dispensationalist camp, but many are not, and they have dominant cult tendencies. Some of these culttendencies become evident by their definition of terms like (The Day of the LORD or calling the martyred people of God "Tribulation Saints)." Their definition of "The Day of the LORD" is the same asthe seven year Tribulation Period. So, they use both terms interchangeably. However, the description of "The Day of the LORD"is as follows:

> *"And the LORD utters His voice before His army; surely His camp is very great, for strong is He who carries out His word. The day of the LORD is indeed great and very awesome, and who can endure it?"* (Joel 2:11 description of "The Day of the LORD).

There are Old Testament Saints and New Testament Saints (who have the New Covenant promise in them)." However, since the Dspensationalist Theology does not allow for the New Testament Saints to be in the Tribulation, they make up a new term like "Tribulation Saints." Then as proof, they say, "See the Church is not mentioned after Revelation chapter 3, so the Church must have already been Raptured!"

The term "Tribulation Saints" agrees with their doctrinal teachings but not with the Bible. We will try to correct some of their other erroneous teachings about end-times, but most notably no one likes to be told they are wrong and need correcting! Amen!

However, remember Cain and his reaction to criticism? However, the problems with much of these end-time teachings errors are significant and must be exposed. Plus, they even discourage the Saints from studying prophecy because of their mantra, "We are not going to be here!" They do not only have to adjust or tweak some of their teaching about end-times, they need to repent of those teaching and radically change all of their time lines and the teachings that follow.

To begin with, most of the Pretribulation End-time Teachings could be destroyed by this one Bible verse:

> *"And there was given to him* (Antichrist) *a mouth speaking arrogant words and blasphemies; and authority* **to act** *for forty-two months was given to him"* (Revelation 13:5).

The question is how long did God give the Antichrist authority to act or when is the Spirit's restraining power removed? At the midpoint of the Tribulation (for forty-two months or three and one- half years), and not (eighty-four months or seven years) like most Dispensation prophecy teachers would have you believe. It is at the halfway mark when the Devil and his demons are thrown down (Revelation 12), and it is at this point that the Antichrist appears on the scene. So, the Antichrist does not start the Tribulation. The Lord Jesus Christ starts the Tribulation when He breaks the first seal sending the White Horse Rider.

"And I saw when the lamb broke one of the seven seals, and I heard one of the four living creatures saying as with a voice of thunder, "Come." And I looked, and behold, a white horse, and he who sat onit had a bow; and a crown was given to him; and he went out conquering, and to conquer" (Revelation6:1-2).

We will discuss later who is the Rider on The White Horse, but we will give you a clue that it is not the Antichrist, False Prophet, Satan or any demon. That is why you have to know and understand the Scriptures, so you will know what God is doing and why?

"Surely the Lord God does nothing unless he reveals His secret counsel to His servants the prophets. A lion has roared! who will not fear? The Lord God has spoken! Who can but prophesy?" (Amos 3:7-8).

Most people, including, many professing Christians, do not understand that Satan is presently the god of this world and in control of all the evil world's systems (including all religions). Satan controls all of the world systems that we mentioned earlier, and that is why Jesus is returning to take back His creation that was lost in the Garden of Eden and won back at the cross.

"And Jesus answered him, "It is written, 'MAN SHALL NOT LIVE ON BREAD ALONE.'" And he led Him up and showed Him all the kingdoms

of the world in a moment of time. And the devil said to Him, "I will give You all this domain and its glory; for it has been handed over to me, and I give it to whomever I wish."Therefore if You worship before me, it shall all be Yours" (Luke 4:4-7).

Please note that Jesus did not dispute Satan's claim to have control of all the kingdoms of this present world, which includes the world's systems. Everything is broken! The world we live in is not heaven, and God wants you to understand that simple fact. Yes, people know it intellectually, but they do not understand it. They are like little children who continuously say, "That's not fair." God never told anyone that life on Earth was fair. Remember: the judge has already declared that you are guilty and how you need a high- powered defense attorney, but again they say, "That's not fair!"

All of us were born behind the proverbial "Eight Ball," and it is everyone's responsibility to get out from behind it and find life's real meaning and purpose. No, this world is not hell, but this world will be as close to heaven that many will ever get. However, looking for peace and order in a broken, chaotic world is troubling and frustrating. People are looking for love, meaning, and purpose, but in all the wrong places. The only place to find peace and love is in the Person of The Lord Jesus Christ.

""Peace I leave with you; My peace I give to you; not as the world gives, do I give to you. let

not your heart be troubled, nor let it be fearful"
(John 14:27).

The peace of God is an inside job and cannot be found
in the physical things of the world. So, please do not get to
comfortable with things down here because all these worldly
things will soon pass away.

*"For all that is in the world, the lust of the
flesh and the lust of the eyes and the boastful
pride of life, is not from the Father, but is from the
world. And the world is passing away, and also its
lusts; but the one who does the will of God abides
forever"* (1 John 2:16-17).

Thus, the Book of the Revelation is the revealing to the
world how the Lord Jesus Christ receives the title deed to the
Earth from His Father. He opens it by breaking the seals, and
He finally comes to Earth and takes control over Satan and
all peoples, tongues, and nations.

*"And they sang a new song, saying, "Worthy art
Thou to take the book, and to break its seals; for
Thou wast slain, and didst purchase for God with
Thy blood men from every tribe and tongue and
people and nation. "And Thou hast made them to
be a kingdom and priests to our God; and they will
reign upon the earth"* (Revelation 5:9-10).

Again, when you read many of today's prophecy books, you would think that the Book of the Revelation is the Revelation of the Devil and not the Revelation of the Lord Jesus Christ. Yes, we will discuss this principle in more detail when we look at Revelation 6.

#8 The Transfiguration

Let us first look at the transfiguration of the Lord. The transfiguration of the Lord Jesus Christ (Matthew 17) was not done to impress the apostles. It was done for our instruction to be encouraged and have perseverance and maintain the blessed hope. Remember it is those who endure to the end who will be saved.

> *"For whatever was written in earlier times was written for our instruction, that through perseverance and the encouragement of the scriptures we might have hope. Now may the God who gives perseverance and encouragement grant you to be of the same mind with one another according to Christ Jesus; that with one accord you may with one voice glorify the God and Father of our Lord Jesus Christ"* (Romans 15:4-6).

At the transfiguration of the Lord (Matthew 17), both Moses and Elijah were present. Thus, three of our significant witnesses were present at the transfiguration. These witnesses are essential characters because they represent the Scriptural Teachings of the Law and the Prophets.

"To the Law and to the testimony (of the Prophets)! If they do not speak according to this word, it is because they have no dawn (Isaiah 8:20).

So, if one does not teach the Law and the testimony of the Scriptural Prophets they have no light and they are in the dark and are spiritually blind.

"While he was still speaking, behold, a bright cloud overshadowed them; and behold, a voice out of the cloud, saying, "This is My beloved Son, with whom I am well-pleased; listen to Him" (Matthew 17:5).

The Father said, "Listen to Him," but the visual (aid) situation was inferring to listen to them who are witnesses to My Son (Moses and Elijah), because they wrote about Him. Listen to all three of them. The key is to listen! Again, the transfiguration proves that neither Moses nor Elijah are coming back. Why is that?

"And when they have finished their testimony, (the two Revelation Prophets) *the beast that comes up out of the abyss will make war with them, and overcome them and kill them. And their dead bodies will lie in the street of the great city which mystically is called Sodom and Egypt, where also their Lord was crucified. And those from the peoples and tribes and tongues and nations will look at their dead bodies for three and a half days,*

and will not permit their dead bodies to be laid in a tomb" (Revelation 11:7-9).

Moses and Elijah have their resurrection bodies (of flesh and bone [like Luke 24:39]), and they cannot die. The Two Prophets in the Book of the Revelation will die, thus proving that neither Moses nor Elijah are coming back down to Earth to die.

They must have their resurrection bodies of flesh and bone because no one who has flesh and blood can see God and live (1 Corinthians 15:50). So, I cannot imagine Moses still asking God if he could see His Face?

> *"Now He (Jesus) said to them, "These are My words which I spoke to you while I was still with you, that all things which are written about Me in the Law of Moses and the prophets and the psalms must be fulfilled." Then He opened their minds to understand the Scriptures, and He said to them, "Thus it is written, that the Christ should suffer and rise again from the dead the third day; and that repentance for forgiveness of sins should be proclaimed in His name to all the nations, beginning from Jerusalem. "You are witnesses of these things. "And behold, I am sending forth the promise of My Father upon you; but you are to stay in the city until you are clothed with power from on high"* (Luke 24:44-49).

Jesus said this to the religious leaders of his day. If you do not believe in the teachings of Moses (the lawgiver), then you would not believe in Me either. Why? Because he wrote about Me.

> ""Do not think that I will accuse you before the Father; the one who accuses you is Moses, in whom you have set your hope. "For if you believed Moses, you would believe Me; for he wrote of Me. "But if you do not believe his writings, how will you believe My words?" (John 5:45-47).

What accuses men before the Father? The Law given to Moses and then given to the people. Again, at the transfiguration, the Father spoke from heaven and said, "Hear Him!"

> "Peter answered and said to Jesus, "Lord, it is good for us to be here; if You wish, I will make three tabernacles here, one for You, and one for Moses, and one for Elijah." While he was still speaking, behold, a bright cloud overshadowed them; and behold, a voice out of the cloud, saying, "This is My beloved Son, with whom I am well-pleased; Hear Him!" (Matthew 17:4-5).

What is the crucial statement of the Father? "This is My beloved Son. "Hear Him!" But again, implied in this statement is the understanding, listen to all my witnesses which includes Moses and Elijah (that are here representing the Law and the

Prophets) because they spoke and wrote about Him. Thus, eliminating a red- letter edition of the Bible where you only listen to what Jesus said and not to the other witnesses. Wake Up, Listen Up, or Go Down!

#9 The Law

One of the major problems in our churches today, (that we already discussed) has to do with the Teachings about the Oraclesof God, which includes the Mosaic Law, Statutes and Ordinances. Many professing Christians in our churches today throw away the Law pieces of the puzzle because they do not fit into their picture, stating "We are not under the Law but under Grace." Most professing Christians (who are primarily Gentiles) have difficultyunderstanding or applying God's Laws, Statutes and Ordinances in their lives.

> *"Remember the law of Moses My servant, even*
> *the statutes and ordinances which I commanded*
> *him in Horeb for all Israel"* (Malachi 4:4).

So, we see that what Moses wrote was for all Israel and they must still keep all of God's Laws, statutes and ordinances. However,Gentiles who want to be saved should voluntarily put themselves under the Law because it can then lead them to salvation in Christ. The Law exposes your sin and reinforces your need for a savior.

> *"Now we know that whatever the Law says,*
> *it speaks to those who are under the Law, that*

every mouth may be closed, and all the world may become accountable to God; because by the works of the Law no flesh will be justified in his sight; for through the Law comes the knowledge of sin" (Romans 3:19- 20).

The Mosaic Law was given to the Jews, but the Law will judge all of humanity, including the Gentiles.

"That every mouth may be closed, and the whole world may become accountable to God" (Romans 3:19b).

You must first put yourself under the Letter of the Law because you will be judged by it (and all the world may become accountable to God). So, shortly after you put yourself under the Law (as a Gentile), you will realize very quickly that you cannot do it. Thus, the question comes, "Why put yourself under it if you cannot do it? Because if you don't put yourself under the Law you will not recognize your sinfulness and you will be one of the foolish *"sayers" that* we talked about in 1 John 1:10.

"If we say that we have not sinned, we make Him a liar, and His word is not in us" (1 John 1:10).

These people say that they have never sinned (even in the past), and thus, they are liars, and they do not have the word of God abiding in them. The purpose of the Law is to show you what a great sinner you are, and when you recognize your utter sinfulness, you will seek the Savior. If one cannot acknowledge their sinfulness; there is no need for a Savior. False teachers will tell pseudo- Christians that they are no longer under Law, but under Grace, but most of them are not saved, and they are still under the judgments of the Letter of the Law.

""Not everyone who says to Me, 'Lord, Lord,' will enter the kingdom of heaven; but he who does the will of My Father who is in heaven. "Many will say to Me on that day, 'Lord, Lord, did we not prophesy in Your name, and in Your name cast out demons, and in Your name perform many miracles?' "And then I will declare to them, 'I never knew you; depart from Me, you who practice lawlessness" (Matthew 7:21- 23).

You must understand this simple fact!

""But when the king came in to look over the dinner guests, he saw there a man not dressed in wedding clothes (the king's righteousness), *And he said to him,' Friend, how did you come in here without wedding clothes?' And he was speechless. "Then the king said to the servants, "Bind him hand and foot, and cast him into the outer darkness; in thatplace there shall be weeping and gnashing of teeth.' "For many are called, but few are chosen"* (Matthew 22:11-14).

Many have heard the gospel preached (they have been called to the wedding feast), but they have not been chosen to receive the king's righteousness (the proper wedding garments).

> *"For many are called, but few are chosen"* (Matthew 22:14).

Remember, sin is lawlessness, but if you practice lawlessness (sin) it means you are unsaved, and you are still under the Letter of the Law. Sin is a theological term. It is when a person breaks one of God's laws, and thus, they sin against God's holiness. David tells us against whom he has sinned. Note the apparent absence of either Bathsheba or Uriah?

> *"For I know my transgressions, and my sin is ever before me. Against Thee, Thee only, I have sinned, and done what is evil in Thy sight, so that Thou art justified when Thou dost speak, and blameless when Thou dost judge"* (Psalms 51:3-4).

There are enough laws in the Word of God to condemn you, so do not add to your condemnation by making things sinful that are not sinful. E.g.; The drinking of alcoholic beverages is not sinful, but if you believe that it is sinful, and you do drink, you are sinning! Why? Because if you believe it is sinful, and you have a drink, then you are acting against your conscience and that is a sin. What is even worse is when your church or synagogue teachings make you sin when there is no sin. Some churches loosely teach not to eat meat on Fridays, but if one of their people believes it to be a sin and they eat meat on Friday, guess what? Sin! Why is it sin? Because they did not live up to what they believed to be true. The same principle applies to the Jews and eating kosher. Yes, there are many dietary restrictions, but combining dairy and meat products are not one of them.

> *"You shall not boil a kid in its mother's milk"* (Exodus 34:26b).

You are not to add or take away from the Book of the Law.

> *""And now, O Israel, listen to the statutes and the judgments which I am teaching you to perform, in order that you may live and go in and take possession of the land which the Lord, the God of your fathers, is giving you. You shall not add to the word which I am commanding you, nor take away from it, that you may keep the commandments of the Lord your God which I command you"* (Deuteronomy 4:1-3).

So, when it says you shall not boil a kid in its mother's milk, it means nothing more than that. However, if you believe that the kosher teachings must be observed; then you must keep kosher perfectly because if you do not, you are guilty of sin. Why? Because you went against what you believed to be true, and as you judge, you will be judged.

> *"Therefore, to one who knows the right thing to do, and does not do it, to him it is sin"* (James 5:17).

So, the bottom line is to know what is and what is not sin. One is to be a Biblical Jew/Christian and not a cultural Jew/Christian. A cultural Christian believes that drinking, dancing, gambling, smoking,eating certain foods, going into a bowling alley and other externals are sinful. They falsely believe that there is sin and a devil behind every rock and bush. So, if one believes any of the cultural taboos tobe sinful (even though they are not), if they do them, they sinbecause they acted against their conscience. Also, cultural Christians use the cultural taboos as their way of bragging about their external righteousness before men when they abstain.

> *"For the kingdom of God is not eating and drinking, but righteousness and peace and joy in the Holy Spirit"* (Romans 14:17).

So, if you are really under the New Covenant, then there are no external laws to break. If there are no laws to break, you cannot sin. This same principle is true regarding man's laws. Sinful men must also keep man's laws to the letter, but if you are under the New Covenant, you function under the Spirit of the Law even when it pertains to man's laws.

> *"For sin shall not be master over you, for you are not under law, but under grace. What then? Shall we sin because we are not under law but under grace? May it never be!"* (Romans 6:14-15).

The key is if you are saved, you are saved from your sins (and thus sin shall not be master over you).

"Come now, and let us reason together," says the Lord, "Though your sins are as scarlet, they will be as white as snow; though they are red like crimson, they will be like wool. "If you consent and obey, you will eat the best of the land; "but if you refuse and rebel, you will be devoured by the sword." Truly, the mouth of the Lord has spoken" (Isaiah1:18-20).

A saved person can be tempted, but he has power over sin. If he does something that appears to be sinful by men, it is because that individual might be showing that he loves himself more than he loves God or that he is not saved in the first place.

"You shall receive power when the Holy Spirit hascome upon you;..." (Acts 1:8).

When one walks in the Spirit, they will not carry out the deeds of the flesh. Thus, the need for spiritual maturity. One is no longer a slave to sin because he is free from sin, and the Son has set him free. He is a new creature in Christ (2 Corinthians 5:17).

"For by one offering he has perfected for all time those who are sanctified. And the Holy Spirit also bears witness to us; for after saying,"THIS IS THE COVENANT THAT I WILL MAKE WITH THEM AFTER THOSE DAYS, SAYS THE LORD: I WILL PUT MY LAWS UPON THEIR HEART, AND UPON THEIR MIND

I WILL WRITE THEM," He then says, "AND THEIR SINS AND THEIR LAWLESS DEEDS I WILL REMEMBER NO MORE" (Hebrews 10:14-17).

A sinner sins because he has a sin nature and does what comes naturally to him – sinful thoughts, sinful words, and sinful deeds. Conversely, what comes naturally to a Saint (a Holy One) is righteous thinking and righteous behavior.

> *Little children, let no one deceive you. He who does right is righteous, as He is righteous. He who commits sin is of the devil; for the devil has sinned from the beginning. The reason the Son of God appeared was to destroy the works of the devil. No one born of God commits sin; for God's nature abides in him, and he cannot sin because he is born of God.*

> *By this it may be seen who are the children of God, and who are the children of the devil: whoever does not do right is not of God, nor he who does not love his brother (1 John 3:7-10 RSV).*

> *"For sin shall not be master over you, for you are not under law, but under grace"* (Romans 6:14).

Sin will not be a master over the Saints, because they are masters over it, and they are also masters over all the works of the Devil.

"We are from God; he who knows God listens to us; he who is not from God does not listen to us. By this we know the spirit of truth and the spirit of error" 1 John 4:6

Yes, sinners may claim they are not under law, but their claims may be false. They are claiming something that is Biblical for the people of The Way; but sinners are not free from the curse of the Law and that is why they are lawless.

"Beloved, while I was making every effort to write you about our common salvation, I felt the necessity to write to you appealing that you contend earnestly for the faith which was once for all delivered to the saints. For certain persons have crept in unnoticed, those who were long beforehand marked out for this condemnation, ungodly persons who turn the grace of our God into licentiousness (disregard for accepted rules and standards – lawlessness) and deny our only Master and Lord, Jesus Christ" (Jude 3-4).

A further misunderstanding of the principles of Law comes from what Paul said about the tutor.

"Therefore the Law has become our tutor to lead us to Christ, that we may be justified by faith. Butnow that faith has come, we are no longer under a tutor" (Galatians 3:24-25).

When Paul is talking about the Law, he is referring to the Letter of the Law (that kills) and not the Spirit of the Law (that gives life). (We will explain the Spirit of the Law in a little more detail when we talk about the Sabbath). A tutor is a teacher who gives individual instruction to a student. Paul tells us about his tutoring of Timothy and Timothy's other tutors.

> *"I thank God, whom I serve with a clear conscience the way my forefathers did, as I constantly remember you in my prayer's night and day, longing to see you, even as I recall your tears, so that I may be filled with joy. For I am mindful of the sincere faith within you, which first dwelt in your grandmother Lois, and your mother Eunice, and I am sure that it is in you as well"* (2 Timothy 1:3-5).

So, Paul mentions three of Timothy's tutors. His mother Eunice, his grandmother Lois and Paul himself. They taught Timothy one of the elementary principles of the oracles of God, which is faith, and we know that without faith, it is impossible to please God (Hebrews 11:6).

> *"Therefore leaving the elementary teaching about the Christ, let us press on to maturity, not laying again a foundation of repentance from dead works and of faith toward God,"* (Hebrews 6:1).

Faith toward God is an elementary tutor teaching principle, and one has to get beyond even that simple starting point and press on to maturity. Most of us never had private tutors because we attended a public/private school system. So, you can think of the public or private school system as a tutor for your fifth-grade students. You could add years to that, but they generally call those first five grades an elementary school.

So, what do tutors, or elementary school teachers do or teach? The first thing you learn or principle you understand is that you can trust them, and they are looking out for your good. You believe that you can trust them and what they are teaching you is correct. You learn to have faith in your teachers. Accordingly, no matter what introductory courses they are teaching (reading, writing, math, English, history, and the like), you believe they are teaching you accurate information.

The child is believing and has no doubt (Matthew 19:14); they think that their tutors are honest and that they are being taught the truth.

> *"Therefore the Law has become our tutor to lead us to Christ, that we may be justified by faith. But now that faith has come, we are no longer under a tutor,...."* (Galatians 3:24-25).

So, what are we saying? You cannot throw out the elementary principles you learned from your parents and your tutors just because you graduated to a higher grade. Faith, along with the Law principles of right and wrong, good and evil are elementary and foundational. That is what one learns from the elementary Law principles. You know right from wrong and good from evil by comparison with the Law. Thus, your beliefs and your actions are determined by what is the final authority in your life. Is the word of God the final authority in your life? What is your final authority? Is it your thinking (Proverbs 3:5-7), your feelings, the teachings of your church, or your friends? I hope for your sake that your answer is theword of God, so you can honestly know what is right and what is wrong thinking and behavior.

> *"Therefore the Law has become our tutor to leadus to Christ, that we may be justified by faith. Butnow that faith has come, we are no longer under a tutor"* (Galatians 3:24-25).

When you break the Letter of the Law, you realize you need a Savior to save you from your (now exposed) sins, and the way to accept that Savior is through faith. Paul further states that when Saving Faith comes, we are no longer under the Letter of the Law. Yes, we graduated, and we are no longer under the tutor (theLetter), but we must remember the principles that our tutors taught us (Proverbs 22:6). These principles get written on our hearts, and they become part of who we are and how we think. As such, a good teacher will continuously remind their students of the elementary principles, that they already know but might need some refreshing.

Peter put it this way;

> *"Therefore, I shall always be ready to remind you of these things, even though you already know*

them, and have been established in the truth which is present with you" (2 Peter 1:12).

You cannot throw away the Spirit of the Law that has been written on your heart.

""This is the covenant that I will make with them after those days, says the Lord: I will put my Laws upon their heart, and upon their mind I will write them," He then says, "AND THEIR SINS AND THEIR LAWLESS DEEDS I WILL REMEMBER NO MORE" (Hebrews 10:16-17).

Pseudo Christians falsely believe they are not under the Letter of the Law, but they are. They were never saved, and they prove that fact by continuing to sin. They do not follow their conscience, nor do they listen to the Spirit of the Law that is written on a believer's heart. They do not live by faith because they do not live up to what they know is right.

"Therefore, to one who knows the right thing to do, and does not do it, to him it is sin" (James 4:17).

Remember that sin is lawlessness. If one is Genuinely Under Grace, they would not and could not sin. Why? Because the only way anyone can sin is by breaking one of God's Laws. If there are no Laws to break (Grace), then there is no violation of Law and therefore no sin.

"For the Law brings about wrath, but where thereis no Law, neither is there violation" (Romans 4:15).

"Everyone who commits sin is guilty of lawlessness; sin is lawlessness. You know that He appeared to take away sins, and in Him there is no sin. No one who abides in Him sins; no one who sins has either seen Him or known Him. Little children, letno one deceive you. He who does right is righteous, as he is righteous. He who commits sin is of thedevil; for the devil has sinned from the beginning. The reason the Son of God appeared was to destroy the works of the devil. No one born of God commits sin; for God's nature abides in him, and he cannot sin because he is born of God. By this it may be seen who are the children of God, and who are the children of the devil: whoever does not do right is not of God, nor he who does not love his brother" (1 John3:4-10 RSV).

The Revised Standard Version (RSV) verse 9 should drive those who believe that the Saints still have the sin nature to their knees. The Revised Standard Version (RSV) is the best translation here because the New American Standard (NASB) adds the word *practices* and the New International Version (NIV) adds the word *continually*. Neither word should be added to the text because neither word gives the text clarity. Do you have to be continually and habitually practicing sin

(24/7) to qualify as being a sinner? No! Because, one is a sinner by nature and not a sinner because he sins! The sinner only does what comes naturally to him, which is sinful behavior.

"No one born of God commits sin; for God's nature abides in him, and he cannot sin because he is born of God" (1 John 3:9).

Let's break down the verse. *No one* (means without exception -- universal truth) who is *born of God* (who is born again from above) *sins*. Why can't a born-again believer sin? Because God's Divine Nature abides in him.

"He who commits sin is of the devil; for the devil has sinned from the beginning. The reason the son of God appeared was to destroy the works of the devil. No one born of God commits sin; for God's nature abides in him, and he cannot sin because he is born of God" (1 John 4:8-9).

There is one thing that God cannot do and that is to sin. He is Holy (meaning without sin), and if we (as children and Saints) have His Divine Nature, then we cannot sin either. The liberals in the United States treat the Bible like they do the Constitution of the United States. They believe the Constitution of the United States of America was a document written by men but not complete nor up to date. They feel they have the right to change it to their liking. They do the same thing with the Bible. They say it was written thousands of years ago (thus outdated) by men (and not God inspired) and that they (The New Liberal Thinkers) have the right to change the Bible to their liking. Wrong, because they end up denying God, and they make God in their image rather than them being made in the image of God.

> *"For the wrath of God is revealed from heaven against all ungodliness and unrighteousness of men, who suppress the truth in unrighteousness, because that which is known about God is evident within them; for God made it evident to them. For since the creation of the world His invisible attributes, his eternal power and divine nature, have been clearly seen, being understood through what has been made, so that they are without excuse. For even though they knew God, they did not honor Him as God, or give thanks; but they became futile in their speculations, and their foolish heart was darkened. Professing to be wise, they became fools, and exchanged the glory of the incorruptible God for an image in the form of corruptible man and of birds and four-footed animals and crawling creatures"* (Romans 1:18-23).

The Law was given to tell us how bad we are and not how good we are. The Law was given to show us how short we fall from perfection and to tell us why we need a Savior. We need a Savior to save us from our sin nature that causes us to sin.

> *"Now we know that whatever the Law says, it speaks to those who are under the Law, that every mouth may be closed, and all the world may become accountable to God; because by the*

works of the Law no flesh will be justified in his sight; for through the Law comes the knowledge of sin" (Romans 3:19- 20).

Through the Law comes the knowledge of sin, and the Law makes us accountable to God. That is why Law must be preached and obeyed. No flesh has been or will be justified by the works of the Law. The Law only makes us accountable to God as a guilty sinner who needs a Savior. The Law is an essential aspect of the gospel message. Why? Before one accepts The Lord Jesus Christ as Savior they are under the Letter of the Law. Whether they believe it or not or whether they are Jewish or not. All have sinned and fall short of the glory of God.

"For as in Adam all die" (1 Corinthians 15:22).

"Now we know that whatever the Law says, it speaks to those who are under the Law, that every mouth may be closed, and all the world may become accountable to God; because by the works of the Law no flesh will be justified in his sight; for through the Law comes the knowledge of sin" (Romans 3:19- 20).

Thus, all humanity must fulfill all aspects of God's Laws, given to men by God. However, the Law aspect of the gospel is being neglected today. Our churches are not teaching Law. They jump right into a Grace Teaching, and people do not even know what Salvation means. Salvation means you are being saved – from the curse of the Law. If you do not keep the Law perfectly (100% of the time), you are cursed and going down. Wake Up, Listen Up or GoDown!

> *"For as many as are of the works of the Law are under a curse; for it is written, "Cursed is everyone who does not abide by all things written in the book of the Law, to perform them." Now that no one is justified by the Law before God is evident; for, "The righteous man shall live by faith." However, the Law is not of faith; on the contrary, "He who practices them shall live by them." Christ redeemed us from the curse of the Law, having become a curse for us-- for it is written, "Cursed is everyone who hangs on a tree"–* (Galatians 3:10-13).

Many pseudo-Christians say they are saved because they had a spiritual experience. However, true born-again believers do not rely on a one-time experience for salvation. When the rebirth is legitimate, the Holy Spirit would be continually leading, directing, and guiding them daily throughout their lives.

> *"For all who are being* (presently) *led by the Spirit of God, these are sons of God"* (Romans 8:14).

All those who are presently (moment by moment) being led by the Spirit of God, these are the sons of God. Salvation is not a one- time experience. Salvation is a Spirit-led Spirit-controlled life.

> *"The Spirit Himself bears witness with our spirit that we are children of God, and if children, heirs also, heirs of God and fellow heirs with Christ, if indeed we suffer with Him in order that we may also be glorified with Him"* (Romans 8:16-17).

Many of the people who claim to be saved never experienced the changes that a true son of God would go through.

> *"Therefore, putting aside all malice and all guile and hypocrisy and envy and all slander, like newborn babes, long for the pure milk of the word, that by it you may grow in respect to salvation, if you have tasted the kindness of the Lord. And coming to Him as to a living stone, rejected by men, but choice and precious in the sight of God, you also, as living stones, are being built up as a spiritual house for a holy priesthood, to offer up spiritual sacrifices acceptable to God through Jesus Christ"*(1 Pet.2:1-5).

First off, you will notice that one gets both their speech and their actions under control, then they have a desire to know God and His Word as much as a baby wants to drink milk. Your desire is to grow up and be strong in the faith (concerning salvation), and if you did not grow up, it was because you did not drink your milk! Peter is saying the same thing spiritually that your mother told you, "If you want to grow up and be strong, you have to drink your milk!" The people of God have inquiring minds. The more one knows about God; the more one wants to know. Moses wanted to see God's Face (Exodus 33:17-23). Paul wanted to know and experience what Jesus knew and experienced!

> *"Not having a righteousness of my own derived from the Law, but that which is through faith in Christ, the righteousness which comes from God on the basis of faith, That I may know Him, and the power ofHis resurrection and the fellowship of His sufferings, being conformed to His death; In order that I may attain to the resurrection from the dead"* (Philippians 3:9-11).

The Jewish leaders of Jesus day believed they were righteous (right) with God, but Jesus told them otherwise.

> *"And Jesus said, "For judgment I came into this world, that those who do not see may see; and that those who see may become blind." Those of the pharisees who were with Him heard these things, and said to Him, "We are not blind too, are we?" Jesus said to them, "If you were blind, you would have no sin; but since you say, 'We see,' your sin remains"* (John 9:39-41).

You have to ask the question, "Why did the Jewish leadership hate Jesus and want to kill Him? The answer is

His Gospel Messageto them about the Law and their sin (also known as lawlessness).

> ""*Did not Moses give you the Law, and yet none ofyou carries out the Law? Why do you seek to kill Me?" The multitude answered, "You have a demon! Who seeks to kill You?"* (John 7:19-24).

He was telling them that according to the Law given to them by Moses that their deeds were evil (their deeds were like the deeds of Cain—evil) but in contrast Christ's words and deeds were righteous.

> ""*Which one of you convicts Me of sin? If I speak truth, why do you not believe Me? "He who is of God hears the words of God; for this reason you do not hear them, because you are not of God"* (John 8:46- 47).

If you want to be part of the persecuted people of God, say what Jesus said to the so-called spiritual leaders. Jesus was saying, "None of you can convict Me of any sin, and I know and speak the truth, but you do not know or understand the truth because you are not of God." You are not saved, and you are not only blind but you are also deaf.

> "'*He who has an ear, let him hear what the Spirit says to the churches. To him who overcomes, I will grant to eat of the tree of life, which is in the paradise of God"* (Revelation 2:7).

When you tell people that their deeds are evil and your deeds are righteous in God's sight, you will get persecuted even by the religious leaders (wolves in sheep's clothing).

> *"There is none righteous, not even one; there is none who understands, there is none who seeks for God; all have turned aside, together they have become useless; there is none who does good, there is not even one"* (Romans 3:11-12).

After you put your faith in Christ, you do get His righteousness (all of it and not just some of it); thus, you are righteous, and you act righteously before God and man.

> *""And this is the judgment, that the light is come into the world, and men loved the darkness rather than the light; for their deeds were evil. "For everyone who does evil hates the light, and does not come to the light, lest his deeds should be exposed. "But he who practices the truth comes to the light, that his deeds may be manifested as having been wrought in God"* (John 3:19 -21).

No one is good except God alone, but He gives His goodness (righteousness) to whomever He wishes. So, when someone says toyou that *"Nobody's Perfect,"* they are making a false universal statement. They don't know *everybody* even to make such a dumb statement. Plus, since they are not perfect themselves, they falsely (judge) and assume that nobody is perfect, and that everyone is a sinner like them.

It is incredible how two groups can hear the same thing and come to opposite conclusions. When one group says, "Nobody's Perfect," they think they have a *good* excuse for continuing in their sinful ways. The other group hears the same words that, "Nobody's Perfect" and they hear a confessed sinner saying the same thing about themselves that God says, "*All have sinned and fall short of the glory of God,*" because "Nobody's Perfect." This is the way Jesus put it to His listeners in John 8:54-55:

> "*Jesus answered, "If I glorify Myself, My glory is nothing; it is my Father who glorifies Me, of whom you say, 'He is our God'; and you have not come to know Him, but I know Him; and if I say that I do not know Him, I shall be a liar like you, but I do know Him, and keep His word.*"

"This is the statement of all genuine people of God. We glorify the Son, and if we say we do not know Him we would be liars, but because we do know Him, intimately and personally, we love Him, and we keep His word.

> "*How long will you keep us in suspense? If you are the Christ, tell us plainly.*" *Jesus answered them, "I told you, and you do not believe; the works that I do in my Father's name, these bear witness of Me.* "*But you do not believe, because you are not of my sheep.* "*My sheep hear My voice, and I know them, and they follow Me; and I give eternal life to them, and they shall never perish; and no one shall snatch them out of My hand.*"My*

Father, who has given them to Me, is greater than all; and no one is able to snatch them out of the Father's hand. "I and the Father are one" (John 10:24-30).

Remember that they hated Jesus without a cause, and they will hate His disciples. Why? Because sinners will react as Cain reacted. They are so deceived and blinded that they believe they are righteous and that the Spirit-filled people of God are the evil ones. They think we are raining on their parade of sin and they want us to shut up or they will shut us up. They have no discernment because of their spiritual blindness, and they do not even know the differencebetween God's children and the Devil's children, which is obvious and evident to any objective observer.

"By this the children of God and the children of thedevil are obvious: anyone who does not practice righteousness is not of God, nor the one who does not love his brother. For this is the message which you have heard from the beginning, that we should love one another; not as Cain, who was of the evil one, and slew his brother. And for what reason did heslay him? Because his deeds were evil, and his brothers were righteous" (1 John 3:10-12).

"For not even His brothers were believing in Him. Jesus therefore said to them, "My time is not yet at hand, but your time is always opportune. "The world cannot hate you; but it hates Me

because I testify ofit, that its deeds are evil" (John 7:5-7).

When you tell people that they are evil in God's sight with Biblical quotes like, *"All have sinned and fall short of the glory of God,"* they become livid. Even many professing Christians become livid when you tell them they are to sin no more. Jesus told the woman caught in adultery and the paralyzed man to sin no more, and they did not even have the indwelling Spirit of God, when He said that to them.

The wolves in sheep's clothing claim to have the Spirit of God, but their sinful deeds prove otherwise. You will know them by their deeds (Matthew 7:16-20). What is "amazing" is the facts that many professing Christians pride themselves on being sinners. They say something like this, *"Christians aren't perfect but forgiven."* They say that so they can justify their sinful behavior. No Christians are perfect because they have been forgiven. They are lights to the, world and they are to let their light shine in such a way that not only believers will see their good works, but non-believers will also see them and glorify your Father who is in heaven.

> *"Let your light shine before men in such a way that they may see your good works, and glorify your Father who is in heaven"* (Matthew 5:16).

Some professing Christians also make oxymoron statements like "I'm a sinner saved by grace." No, if you are a sinner, you are not saved, and you are a mission field to the people of The Way. The question becomes, "From what are you saved?" Your sin. If you are free from your sin and your sin nature, you are no longer a slave to sin (you are free, and you do not have to sin nor do you want to sin).

> *"Jesus answered them, "Truly, truly, I say to you, everyone who commits sin is the slave of sin. "And the slave does not remain in the house forever; the son does remain forever. "If therefore the Son shall make you free, you shall be free indeed. (John 8:34).*

So, if you keep on sinning after coming to the knowledge of the truth, it is willful, and you prove that you do not love the Lord with your whole heart, soul, mind, and strength. You are nothing but a lying hypocrite. However, in contrast to the lying sinners, there are the saved and pure in heart.

> *"Blessed are the pure in heart, for they shall see God"* (Matthew 5:8).

> *"To the pure, all things are pure; but to those who are defiled and unbelieving, nothing is pure, but both their mind and their conscience are defiled. They profess to know God, but by their deeds they deny Him, being detestable and disobedient, and worthless for any good deed"* (Titus 1:15-16).

Saints (Holy Ones) are saved, and they are the pure in heart, but the sinners are the defiled, the blind and the unsaved ones. Sin or the absence of sin is what separates sinners from Saints (Holy Ones).

> *"Every one who commits sin is guilty of lawlessness; sin is lawlessness. You know that He appeared to take away sins, and in Him there is no sin. No one who abides in Him sins; no one who sins has either seen Him or known Him. Little children, let no one deceive you. he who does right is righteous, as He is righteous. He who commits sin is of the devil; for the devil has sinned from the beginning. The reason the Son of God appeared was to destroy the works of the devil. No one born of God commits sin; for God's nature abides in him, and he cannot sin because he is born of God. By this it may be seen who are the children of God, and who are the children of the devil: whoever does not do right is not of God, nor he who does not love his brother"* (1 John 3:4-10).

Without holiness (sanctification), you will not be with the Lord.

You will not get into the Kingdom of God.

> *"Blessed are the pure in heart, for they shall see God,…."* (Matthew 5:8).

> *"Pursue peace with all men, and the sanctification (holiness) without which no one will see the Lord. See to it that no one comes short of the*

grace of God; that no root of bitterness springing up causes trouble, and by it many be defiled; that there be no immoral or godless person like Esau,...." (Hebrews 12:14-16).

Many of these professing Christians are apostates. They know the truth, but they don't walk in it. They call Jesus Lord, but they do not do what he says. They think all they have to do is confess and say they are sorry, but they better remember that godless person named Esau.

"That there be no immoral or godless person like Esau, who sold his own birthright for a single meal.

For you know that even afterwards, when he desired to inherit the blessing, he was rejected, for he found no place for repentance, though he sought for it with tears" (Hebrews 12:16-17).

Esau was immoral and godless, but he was also guilty of neglect. He did not take his God-given responsibility of being the first born seriously. To whom much is given much is expected!

"For this reason we must pay much closer attention to what we have heard, lest we drift away from it. For if the word spoken through angels proved unalterable, and every transgression anddisobedience received a just recompense, how

shall we escape if we neglect so great a salvation?"
(Hebrews 2:1-3).

What are the deeds that these sinners are doing? They are doing sinful deeds of lawlessness?

> *For in the case of those who have once beenenlightened and have tasted of the heavenly gift and have been made partakers of the Holy Spirit, and have tasted the good word of God and the powers of the age to come, and then have fallen away, it is impossible to renew them again to repentance, since they again crucify to themselves the Son of God, and put Him to open shame.* (Hebrews 6:4-6)

You could ask them, "What person or group of people do you know that cannot be renewed again to repentance? Neglectful people like Esau! However, the false teachers will give you some flimsy cultural interpretation. However, in reality, those Scriptures may be talking about them and to them.

> *"For this reason we must pay much closer attention to what we have heard, lest we drift away from it. For if the word spoken through angels provedunalterable, and every transgression and disobedience received a just recompense, how shall we escape if we neglect so great a salvation?"* (Hebrews 2:1-3).

How will one escape the judgment of God if one neglects so great a salvation? When you preach holiness and perfection, you will be hated for that. Sinners do not like to be told that they are spiritually blind and deaf and that their present thinking and behavior is worthy of death. They even get angrier when you tell them you are a Saint (Holy and Pure), but they are practicing lawlessness (for sin is lawlessness). Many of them even believe that they are saved Christians, and they cannot be unsaved no matter how evil their deeds. That is why you cannot bring them again to repentance, because they will tell you that they already did that?

> *"For if after they have escaped the defilements of the world by the knowledge of the Lord and Savior Jesus Christ, they are again entangled in them and are overcome, the last state has become worse for them than the first. For it would be better for them not to have known the way of righteousness, than having known it, to turn away from the holy commandment delivered to them. It has happened to them according to the true proverb, "A dog returns to its own vomit," and, "A sow, after washing, returns to wallowing in the mire"* (2 Peter 2:20-22).

Again, you will know them by their fruit. Good trees produce good fruit, and bad trees produce bad fruit.

> *"And this is the judgment, that the light is come into the world, and men loved the darkness rather than the light; for their deeds were evil.*

"For everyone who does evil hates the light, and does not come to the light, lest his deeds should be exposed. "But he who practices the truth comes to the light, that his deeds may be manifested as having been wrought in God" (Jn. 3:19-21).

Preachers have to be particularly careful of preaching Grace without Law because of the teachings and warnings of Jesus.

""Do not think that I came to abolish the Law or the prophets; I did not come to abolish, but to fulfill. "For truly I say to you, until heaven and earth pass away, not the smallest letter or stroke shall pass away from the Law, until all is accomplished. "Whoever then annuls one of the least of these commandments, and so teaches others, shall be called least in the kingdom of heaven; but whoever keeps and teaches them, he shall be called great in the kingdom of heaven" (Matthew 5:17-19).

If you annul even one of His commandments, and so teaches others, about Grace and how the Law of Moses is abolished, you will be called least in the Kingdom of Heaven. Yes, you might be saved, and you might even have helped others get saved, but your efforts and rewards in heaven will not be what you might think! Why? Because you were preaching a watered-down Gospel because you were fearful of being persecuted for telling people how sinful they are in God's sight.

You are to teach the Letter of the Law to all men to free them from the curse of the Law through faith in The Lord Jesus Christ. However, pastors must (also remind) and teach the Spirit of the Law, even to the people of The Way. Because the Spirit of the Law is not abolished. It is one of the elementary principles that you learned as a child, and you cannot lose or forget those elementary principles of faith, knowing right from wrong, and knowing good and evil. You still must keep and teach the Spirit of the Law. Thus, if you teach the Letter of the Law and remind them of what the Spirit of the Law teaches, you shall be called great in the Kingdom of Heaven. It is necessary to preach the Letter of the Law to unsaved sinners and the Spirit of the Law (as a reminder) to those who have believed. Because it is obvious that the people of God are not to steal, covet, dishonor their parents, and the like.

> *"For when Gentiles* (believers) *who do not have the* (Letter of the) *Law do instinctively the things of the Law* (the Spirit of the Law), *these, not having the* (Letter of the) *Law, are a Law to themselves, in that they show the work of the Law written in their hearts, their conscience bearing witness, and their thoughts alternately accusing or else defending them, on the day when, according to my gospel, God will judge the secrets of men through Christ Jesus"* (Rom. 2:14-16).

We only do away with the Letter of the Law of Moses, when we have the Holy Spirit who writes the Spirit of the Law on our hearts.

> *"Moreover, I will give you a new heart and put a new spirit within you; and I will remove the heart of stone from your flesh and give you a heart of flesh. "And I will put My Spirit within you and cause you to walk in My statutes, and you will be careful to observe My ordinances." (Ezekiel 36:26-27).*

We show the spiritual law written in our hearts. Our conscience via the Spirit becomes our guide. We become a Law unto ourselves, and we pursue excellence. Yes, we seek perfect righteousness, but if we fall short of perfect righteousness, that is when Grace fills in the gap. Example: If you go to school hoping to just get by with a "C," you will probably end up failing. However, if you go into class prepared, and reaching for an "A," you may fall short of the teacher's perfect standard and get a "B." However, because of God's Grace, the teacher's "B" may have been the best you could have done, and God will view that teacher's "B" as His "A." The parable of the talents will help one understand the above illustration (Matthew 25:14ff). Remember to whom much is given much is expected.

First, let us explain the Letter of the Law by example. The Law says, "Thou shalt not steal. "There are no qualifiers like "Grand Theft" or "Petty Larceny." The Law says, "Thou shalt not steal (anything)." That is the Letter of the Law. If you have stolen anythingin your life no matter how small, you are guilty of sin by breaking God's Law and thus being lawless. That being said, that means everyone (just in the area of stealing – all) are guilty because everyone has taken something that did not belong to them at some point in their life (and be reminded that coveting also amounts to stealing). Another example of the Letter of the Law is keeping the Sabbath.

#10 The Sabbath

"Remember the sabbath day, to keep it holy. Six days you shall labor and do all your work, but the seventh day is a sabbath of the Lord your God; in it you shall not do any work, you or your son or your daughter, your male or your female servant or your cattle or your sojourner who stays with you. For in six days the LORD *made the heavens and the earth, the sea and all that is in them, and rested on the seventh day; therefore, the* LORD *blessed the sabbath day and made it holy* (Exodus 20:8-11).

The Letter of the Law states, "You shall not do any work" on the Sabbath. You cannot say to yourself, "God will understand." No, God will not understand. The only thing that God will understands is that you are lawless. His command (Law) is to work six days and rest on the seventh. So, what is the Spirit of the Law for the peopleof The Way (the Spirit-filled Believers)? The elementary principle of the Law is that God does not want you to work seven days a week. Your body and mind need to rest for the sake of your health andyour productivity. You were not made to work seven days a week, God created your body, and He knows that you need one day's rest out of seven.

> *"And He was saying to them, "The Sabbath was made for man, and not man for the Sabbath. "Consequently, the Son of Man is Lord even of the Sabbath"* (Mark 2:27-28).

The Sabbath was made for you to rest. God wants you to have a day off from what you do the other six days. According to the Letter of the Law it has to be on Saturday, but according to the Spirit of the Law, it could be any one day of the week that you choose (you are a Law unto yourself). So, the Sabbath day rest is for your rest. You can select any day of the week for your rest.

> *"Who are you to judge the servant of another? To his own master he stands or falls; and stand he will, for the Lord is able to make him stand. One man regards one day above another, another regards every day alike. Let each man be fully convinced in his own mind. He who observes the day, observes it for the Lord, and he who eats, does so for the Lord, for he gives thanks to God; and he who eats not, for the Lord he does not eat, and gives thanks to God. For not one of us lives for himself, and not one dies for himself; for if we live, we live for the Lord, or if we die, we die for the Lord; therefore whether we live or die, we are the Lord's. For to this end Christ died and lived again, that He might be Lord both of the dead and of the*

*living. But you, why do you judge your brother?
Or you again, why do you regard your brother
with contempt? For we shall all stand before the
judgment seat of God (Rom 14:4-10).*

So, what if a child of God keeps on working seven days a week, "Does he sin?" No. Why not? Because he is not under the Letter of the Law but the Spirit of the Law.

However, the people of God still have to understand God's Underlying Spiritual Principle that God desires men to rest one day aweek for mans good (for his health and his productivity). The Sabbath's day rest is not for God's benefit, but it is in the best interest of man! You then have to ask the question, "If it is not sinning, are there any consequences for the people of The Way whocontinue to work seven days a week without taking a day's rest. Yes, they will experience poor health and not be as productive as they could be. But there is no breakage of the Law (because they are not under the Letter of the Law, but Grace, and the Spirit of the Law). But the people of The Way have to be reminded of God's elementary principals; like what God did to the Nation of Israel for not letting the land rest once every seven years like the Letter of the Law required.

God threw the Israelites out of the land, so the land was forcedto rest (2 Chronicles 36:20-21 and Daniel 9:1-6). All good farmers agree with God that one cannot plant the same crop year after year without giving rest to the land. The nutrients get depleted, but by leaving the field fallow allows the soil to replenish its nutrients, and then the land will be more productive.

So, when God is talking about the Sabbath rest, He is not talking to the land but to us. Stating that if you want to maintain your health and your productivity, make sure you follow My instructions on keeping the Sabbath rest. The Word of God teaches that people and land need to rest. You do not want God to force you to rest by taking away your health or even taking away that job (your productivity) that keeps you working seven days a week.

Remember; judgment starts with the household of God, and God may not discipline you immediately, or maybe not at all, but time is on His side.

"Those whom I love, I reprove and discipline;
be zealous therefore, and repent (Revelation 3:19).

Thus, that seven-day working child of God should take warning because he places himself in a disobedient position with God, and God knows how to discipline His children.

"He disciplines us for our good, that we may
share His holiness" (Hebrews 12:10).

Reminder about the Sabbath: you must remember that the non-believing Israelites are still under the Letter of the Law and they must not do any work on the Sabbath as the Letter of the Law requires. They must keep Saturday as their Sabbath day rest. However, everything changes if one repents and turns from the Letter of the Law to Grace's Spirit of the

Law. N.B., If you do not have the Indwelling Holy Spirit, you are required to keep the Seventh Day Saturday Sabbath.

> *"For the Law was given through Moses; grace and truth were realized through Jesus Christ. No man has seen God at any time; the only begotten God, who is in the bosom of the Father, He has explained Him" (John 1:17-18).*

#11 THE TWO REVELATION PROPHETS

God tells us that we must listen to *the Prophet* that He is sending. We know that *the Prophet*, like Moses, was the Messiah the Lord Jesus Christ (Acts 3), but most did not listen to Him, and thus there were significant consequences for the nation of Israel (Malachi. 4:4-6). So, they better listen to *The Prophet* that will come in the future (JAMES), the Rider on The White Horse that comes in Jesus's stead.

> *The Lord your God will raise up for you a prophet like me from among you, from your countrymen, you shall listen to him. This is according to all that you asked of the Lord your God in Horeb on the day of the assembly, saying, 'Let me not hear again the voice of the Lord my God, let me not see this great fire anymore, lest I die.' "And the Lord said to me, 'They have spoken well. 'I will raise up a prophet from among **their** countrymen like you, and I will put My words in his mouth, and he shall speak to them all that I commend him. 'And it shall come about that whoever will not listen to My words which he shall*

speak in My name, I myself will require it of him (Deuteronomy 18:15-19).

Neither Moses, the lawgiver, nor Elijah, the effectual prayer, are coming back. Moses said, "God is going to send a Prophet *like* me, so it will not be the lawgiver Moses. Also, remember it was Johnthe Baptist who came in the spirit and power of Elijah, but he was not the reincarnated Elijah, which indicates that "U R2 JOHN" will also come in the spirit and power of Elijah and John the Baptist.

> *The* LORD *your God will raise up for you a prophet like me from among you, from your countrymen, you shall listen to him.* (Deuteronomy 18:15)

In verse 15, that Prophet will come from your countrymen, (a Jew—the Lord Jesus Christ, Acts chapter 3), and you shall listen to Him. However, in verse 18, there is another Prophet mentioned (*that Prophet*) will come from **their** countrymen (a Spirit-filled Gentile Christian), and you better listen to God's word which he shall speak in His name. God says, "I will require it of them if they do not listen to him and obey."

Listen Up or Go Down! God wants you to listen to the Prophets like Moses (**JAMES**) and like Elijah (**U R2 JOHN**). It is not the signs and wonders that these Two Prophets perform that are important! (The judgment signs are only "Trumpet Blasting Attention Grabbers" to get you to Listen Up); what is important is their emphasis on Law and Grace as found in the Scriptures. Remember that "Faith comes by hearing, and hearing by the Word of Christ" (Romans 10:17).

> *"Remember the Law of Moses My servant, even the statutes and ordinances which I commanded him in Horeb for all Israel. "Behold, I am going to send you Elijah the Prophet before the coming of the great and terrible day of the Lord. "And he will restore the hearts of the Fathers to their children, and the hearts of the children to their Fathers, lest I come and smite the land with a curse"* (Malachi. 4:4-6).

Plus, the Pretribulation people have a problem here, because if there was a Pretribulation Rapture than why were not the Two Revelation Prophets taken up in it? Yes, they have answers, buttheir answers are either foolish or unbiblical or both. You have toask, "Who are these two guys that God promised to send **before** theGreat and Terrible Day of the Lord?"

> *"Then the angel who was speaking with me returned, and roused me as a man who is awakened from his sleep. And he said to me, "What do you see?" and I said, "I see, and behold, a lampstand all of gold with its bowl on the top of it, and its seven lamps on it with seven spouts belonging to each of the lamps which are on the top of it; also two olive trees by it, one on the right side of the bowl and the other on its left side." Then I answered and said tothe angel who was speaking with me saying,*

"What are these, my Lord?" So the angel who was speakingwith me answered and said to me, "Do you not know what these are?" And I said, "No, my Lord." Then he answered and said to me, "This is the word of the Lord to Zerubbabel saying, "Not by might nor by power, but by My Spirit,' says the Lord of hosts. 'What are you, O great mountain? Before Zerubbabel you will become a plain; and he will bring forth thetop stone with shouts of "Grace, grace to it!"' Also the word of the Lord came to me saying, "The hands of Zerubbabel have laid the foundation of this house, and his hands will finish it. Then you will know that the Lord of hosts has sent me to you. "For who has despised the day of small things? But these seven will be glad when they see the plumb line in the hand of Zerubbabel-- these are the eyes of the Lord which range to and fro throughout the earth." Then I answered and said to him, "What are these two olive trees on the right of the lampstand and on its left?" And I answered the second time and said to him, "What are the two olive branches which are beside the two golden pipes, which empty the golden oil from themselves?" So he answered me saying, "Do you not know what these are?" And I said, "No, my Lord." Then he said, "These are the two anointed ones, who are standing by the Lord of the whole earth" (Zechariah 4: 1-14).

Who are His two witnesses? These are the two anointed ones (Spirit-filled Christians) that are branches grafted into Israel by faith (Romans 11). That is why one can still say what Jesus said, *"You worship that which you do not know; we worship that which we know, for salvation is from the Jews"* (John 4:22-23).

However, the two witnesses also represent the Churches and will be the final word on the Scriptures. Revelation 11 says these Two Prophets are the Two Olive Trees **and** the Two Lampstands. These are two men filled with the Spirit of God (the two anointed ones), who are standing by the Lord of the whole Earth to do His bidding. Giving the world its final warnings before the Day of the Lord comes.

Remember what they represent. The Law and the Prophets (Law and Grace --- New and Old Testaments/ Covenants), these Two Prophets are also Branches on the Olive Tree (Gentiles graftedinto Judaism—Messianic Jews by Faith), and they also represent the Church(es) — Lampstands (Revelation chapters 1-3).

Please take special note that the verses mentioned earlier in (Zechariah chapter 4) are also talking about the beginning and the end of the building of the temple. These verses should be comparedwith Revelation chapter 11. These Two Prophets are coming in the Spirit and Power of Elijah and Moses, but they will be instrumental ingetting a character like Zerubbabel to start and finish the building of the Temple in Jerusalem.

These Two Prophets will come and give humanity a final warning to repent before Jesus Christ (and His army of angles) judges peoples and lands when *the Day of the LORD* starts. However, the reality is that these Two Prophets will be the *start* of God's judgments on the Earth when the Lord Jesus Christ opens theseals and before the Day *of the LORD* begins. Again, God always warns through His Prophets before He destroys.

> *"If a trumpet is blown in a city will not the people tremble? If a calamity occurs in a city has not the Lord done it? Surely the Lord God does nothing unless He reveals His secret counsel to His servants the prophets. A lion has roared! Who will not fear? The Lord God has spoken! Who can but prophesy?"* (Amos 3:6-8).

The Four Horsemen Judgments are general warning judgments by the Two Prophets sent by God before the Day of the *LORD starts.* However, their judgments are still significant because one-quarter of the Earth's population (close to two billion people) will die or be killed during their ministry and that is even before the Antichrist comes on the scene. The Victory White Horse Rider leads the other Three Horsemen of the Apocalypse. The rest of the horses and their riders only follow the lead of the White Horse Rider.

The Prophet like Elijah, John the Baptist is U R2 JOHN, and he is coming in accordance with the word of the Lord. The Jews of Jesus' day were expecting Two Prophets to come and they were to come **"before"** the Great and Terrible Day of the LORD.

> *"Behold, I am going to send you Elijah the prophet before the coming of the great and terrible day of the Lord"* (Malachi 4:5).

We see this in the question the Jewish leaders asked of John the Baptist.

> *"And this is the witness of John* (the Baptist), *when the Jews sent to him priests and Levites from Jerusalem to ask him, "Who are you?" And he confessed, and did not deny, and he confessed, "I am not the Christ." And they asked him, "What then? Are you Elijah?" And he said, "I am not." "Are you the prophet?" And he answered, "No"* (John 1:19-21).

So, we see by their question to John the Baptist indicates that they were expecting either the Christ, Elijah, or *The Prophet* to come *before* the Lord comes. Jesus told his disciples that John the Baptistwas the man of the Elijah prophecy. John the Baptist of the Elijah prophecy has already occurred, but he did not restore all things. However, the "U R2 JOHN" (Elijah) is coming (future) and he will restore all things."

> *"And his disciples asked Him, saying, "Why then do the scribes say that Elijah must come first?" And He answered and said, "Elijah is coming* (future) *and will restore all things; But I say to*

you, that Elijah already came (past), *and they did not recognize him, but did to him whatever they wished. So also the Son of Man is going to suffer at their hands." Then the disciples understood that He had spoken to them about John the Baptist"* (Matthew 17:10-13).

John the Baptist did not restore all things but the man coming in the future "U R2 JOHN" will. We will first look at why they asked John about Elijah or "The Prophet" like Moses from the Book of Malachi?

> *"Remember the law of Moses My servant, even the statutes and ordinances which I commanded him in Horeb for all Israel* (Malachi 4:4).

Again, God wants all of us to remember the Law of Moses His servant, even the statutes and ordinances that God commanded him to write. He wrote the Letter of the Law on tablets of stone.

> *"Behold, I am going to send you Elijah the prophet before the coming of the great and terrible day of the Lord. "And he will restore the hearts of the fathers to their children, and the hearts of the children to their fathers, lest I come and smite the land with a curse"* (Malachi 4:5-6).

So, the key is that the Jews and all of humanity better listen to what that Prophet like Elijah and John the Baptist (U

R2 JOHN) and that Prophet like Moses and the Lord Jesus Christ (JAMES) says. Listen Up or Go Down!

Two Prophets will still come. One in the Spirit and Power of Elijah and John the Baptist (U R2 JOHN) and one in the Spirit and Power of Moses and Jesus (JAMES). If the world's people do not listen to them, then The Lord Jesus will come and smite the land with a curse (The Day of the LORD). The reason that the world's people will be caught off guard *like a thief in the night* is simply because they will not heed the warnings of all of God's witnesses.

> ""*I have come in my Father's name, and you do not receive Me; if another shall come in his own name, you will receive him. "How can you believe, when you receive glory from one another, and you do not seek the glory that is from the one and only God? "Do not think that I will accuse you before the Father; the one who accuses you is Moses, in whom you have set your hope. "For if you believed Moses, you would believe Me; for he wrote of Me. "But if you do not believe his writings, how will you believe My words"* (John 5:43-47).

Even today, during the Passover meal (the sadder), the Jews leave an empty place setting for the Prophet Elijah. They have the children run to the door to see if Elijah had come, because he must come before the Lord comes/returns. Being at one Jewish sadder was eventful when the children were sent to the door, and the individual next to me said, " *fat chance.*" His response seemed comical at the time, but his response is typical because the Jewish people have been waiting and expecting Elijah to come for some twenty-five hundred years. Most of them have given up looking for Elijah just like they have given up looking for their Messiah "The Prophet" (the deliverer) that is like Moses.

> ""And I will grant authority to My two witnesses, and they will prophesy for twelve hundred and sixty days, clothed in sackcloth." These are the two olive trees and the two lampstands that stand before the Lord of the earth. And if anyone desires to harm them, fire proceeds out of their mouth and devours their enemies; and if anyone would desire to harm them, in this manner he must be killed. These have the power to shut up the sky, in order that rain may not fall during the days of their prophesying; and they have power over the waters to turn them into blood, and to smite the earth with every plague, as often as they desire" (Revelation 11:3-6).

Remember it was Elijah a righteous man who asked God to have the rain stop for three and one-half years, and as a result, God answered his prayer, and there was a famine throughout the Earth (worldwide). God did that as a result of the prayer by a righteous man (Elijah), and God will answer the prayers of (JAMES and U R2 JOHN) who are the Two Prophets of Revelation chapter, 11. God is responding to the Prayers of the Prophets. At this point, the Lord is still not acting independently of His Witnesses/Prophets. As such,

God's human witnesses can activate the Power of God on Earth through Faint, Prayer, The Scriptures and The Holy Spirit.

> *"The effective prayer of a righteous man can accomplish much. Elijah was a man with a nature like ours, and he prayed earnestly that it might not rain; and it did not rain on the earth for three years and six months. And he prayed again, and the sky poured rain, and the earth produced its fruit"* (James 5:16- 18).

Again, take note that God did not close up the sky independently of the request by The Prophet (Elijah). Thus, we see the Power of Prayer, and that is why we all should pray.

> *"Now He was telling them a parable to show that at all times they ought to pray and not to lose heart"* (Luke 18:1).

> *"Pray for the peace of Jerusalem: "May they prosper who love you"* (Psalm 122:6).

We know that The Prophet "like Moses" was the Lord Jesus Christ (Acts chapter 3) and God's command to us was this:

> *"The LORD your God will raise up for you a prophet like me from among you, from your countrymen, you shall listen to him"* (Deuteronomy 18:15).

So, the command to listen to the Law and The Prophets continues to this day. However, God is going to give the world another chance (final warning) by sending two more Prophets. One like Moses (JAMES) and the other like Elijah (U R2 JOHN). Both are coming in the Spirit and Power of those Four Prophets of old.

However, the Two Prophets in the Book of the Revelation chapter 11 will be born again Christians, who not only represent the Law and the Prophets, they are also the Two Lampstands, the Lord's True Church, and the Two Olive Trees that also represent the Nation of Israel. But they are not the reincarnated prophets of old. As such, the Church and the nation of Israel will go through the Tribulation. Remember: The Two Prophets are the Lampstands, and the Lampstands represent the Church(es). So, the Church is not only represented in the Tribulation by the Two Prophets, but the Church will also be in it. God will not take out His witnesses when He can use them the most to get people to repent.

> ""I have given them Thy word; and the world has hated them, because they are not of the world, even as I am not of the world. "I do not ask Thee to take them out of the world, but to keep them from the evil one" (John 17:14-15).

> "I, John, your brother and fellow partaker in the tribulation and kingdom and perseverance which are in Jesus,…." (Revelation 1:9).

#12 Israel And The Church

Israel is presently a nation of unbelieving people; many have been cut off because of their unbelief (Romans 11). The people of God (The True Church) is a nation of believing people.

> "*And, (*to unbelievers—Jesus is) *"A STONE OF STUMBLING AND A ROCK OF OFFENSE"; for they stumble because they are disobedient to the word, and to this doom they were also appointed. But you* (Jews and Gentiles who believe in the Lord Jesus Christ) *are A CHOSEN RACE, A ROYAL PRIESTHOOD, A HOLY NATION, A PEOPLE FOR GOD'S OWN POSSESSION, that you may proclaim the excellencies of Him who has called you out of darkness into His marvelous light; for you* (Gentiles) *once were NOT A PEOPLE, but now you are THE PEOPLE OF GOD; you had NOT RECEIVED MERCY, but now you have RECEIVED MERCY"* (1 Peter 2:8-10).

Today, when a Jewish person truly believes on The Lord Jesus Christ, they are put into the Church (The Body of Christ) by God. However, they are also grafted back into the Olive Tree of Israel because of their faith. It will be the same during the Tribulation. When a non-believer (Jew or Gentile) becomes a believer, he/she is put into the Church – the Body of Christ, and they both are grafted into the Olive Tree of Israel. The bottom line is this:

> *"There is one body and one Spirit, just as also you were called in one hope of your calling; one Lord, one faith, one baptism, one God and Father of all who is over all and through all and in all. But to each one of us grace was given according to the measure of Christ's gift"* (Ephesians. 4:4-7).

You also have to remember this:

> *""And I have other sheep (Gentiles), which are not of this fold (Jews); I must bring them also, and they shall hear My voice; and they shall become one flock with one shepherd"* (John 10:16).

It is the same idea of a united one in Hebrew which is ('echaad - or 'echad (ekh-awd'). It is like in a marriage where two people (the man and woman) are a united "one."

> *"For this cause a man shall leave his Father and his mother, and shall cleave to his wife; and they shall become **one** flesh"* (Genesis 2:24).

The believing Church and believing Israel groups are a united one or even like the trinity where three persons of the Godhead are "one" God.

> ""*Hear, O Israel! the Lord is our God, the Lord is one!*" (Deuteronomy 6:4).

Again the *one* is a united one ""(echaad" or 'echad)" the believing Gentiles are now part of believing Israel (by faith) and the believing Israelites are put into the Church (because of their faith in the Lord). Yes, believing Gentiles are grafted into the Jewish olive tree and believing Jews are put in (or grafted) into the Church. However, it is the one united body of believers in Christ (The Believing Church and Believing Israel) that is the **one** ('echaad) flock shepherded by the Good Shepherd.

> "*For He Himself is our peace, who made both groups into one, and broke down the barrier of the dividing wall, by abolishing in His flesh the enmity, which is the Law of commandments contained in ordinances, that in Himself He might make the two into one new man, thus establishing peace, and might reconcile them both in one body to God through the cross, by it having put to death the enmity*" (Ephesians 2:14-16).

The Church has not replaced non-believers, but the Church has taken in those non-believers who are now believers, and believing Israel has been grafted back into their Natural Olive

Tree. So, both groups are identical (a united one) who all believe like Father Abraham believed.

> *"And if the first piece of dough be holy, the lump is also; and if the root be holy, the branches are too"* (Romans11:16).

All believers (Jews and Gentiles) are called to be, "A *CHOSEN RACE, A ROYAL PRIESTHOOD, A HOLY NATION, A PEOPLE FOR GOD'S POSSESSION, that you may proclaim the excellencies of Him who has called you out of darkness into His marvelous light"* (1 Peter 2:10).

Thus, if it is only believing Israelites that are drafted back into the Olive Tree and the non-believing Israelites remain cut off then this Universal Biblical Statement is true.

> *"That a partial hardening has happened to Israel until the fullness of the Gentiles has come in; Andthus all Israel will be saved; just as it is written, "The deliverer will come from Zion, He will removeungodliness from Jacob." "And this is my covenant with them, when I take away their sins"* (Romans11:25-27).

#13 Who Is This Jesus?

Who is this Jesus? We will now look at the evident when Jesus was asking the disciples who do people say that I am?

> *"Now when Jesus came into the district of Caesarea Philippi, He began asking His disciples, saying, "Who do people say that the Son of Man is?"* (Matthew 16:13).

This is a critical doctrinal question, and Jesus knows it. That is why He asked it to his disciples. Who is the Son of Man? Who is this man asking you this question?

> *And they said, "Some say John the Baptist; and others, Elijah; but still others, Jeremiah, or one of the prophets." He said to them, "But who do you say that I am?"* (Matthew 16:14-15).

He listened to the disciple's answers as to whom people were saying that He was. They were all wrong in their conclusions except one. There is no reincarnation in the Bible, (Hebrews 9:27) but the listeners of Jesus thought he was one of the Prophets who came back to life. That foolish reincarnation thinking was as popular then as it is today. There is another example of a person believing in reincarnation: remember Herod who put John the Baptist to death? He believed that Jesus Christ was the resurrected John the Baptist.

> *"At that time Herod the Tetrarch heard the news about Jesus, and said to his servants, "This is John the Baptist; he has risen from the dead; and that is why miraculous powers are at work in him"* (Matthew 14:1-2).

"Since that thinking was popular, the people thought that Jesus Christ was one of the Resurrected Prophets.

> *"And they said, "Some say John the Baptist; and others, Elijah; but still others, Jeremiah, or one of the prophets." He said to them, "But who do you say that I am?"* (Matthew 16:14).

However, Jesus knew that the people were wrong in their thinking and their confession of Him was in error. He then gets this response from Simon Peter:

> *"And Simon Peter answered and said, "Thou art the Christ, the Son of the living God." And Jesus answered and said to him, "Blessed are you, Simon Barjona, because flesh and blood did not reveal this to you, but My Father who is in heaven"* (Matthew 16:16-17).

Knowing the real Jesus Christ is a gift from the Father. You cannot learn it from men; you get it as a Divine Revelation from the Father.

""No one can come to Me, unless the Father who sent Me draws him; and I will raise him up on the lastday. "It is written in the prophets, 'AND THEY SHALL BE TAUGHT OF GOD.' Everyone who has heard andlearned from the Father, comes to Me" (John 6:44).

Jesus said, I asked you Peter who is the *Son of Man,* and you said, "He is the Christ, and He is the Son of God" He is the God-man—The Lord Jesus Christ. So, what does this mean to us today? You can speculate as to whom Jesus Christ is—a Prophet, a Priest, a King, an Angel, a Good Man, a Good Teacher, a Reincarnated Prophet, a Reincarnated Guru, or a Reincarnated Master, etc.

However, you will not know who He is—the Second Person of the Trinity, the Word of God—until the Spirit of God makes it known to you in your heart. When you are born again from above, you get and have the assurance that your sins are forgiven. Your Spiritual Eyes will be opened, and you will see clearly and Understand Spiritual Things.

"I am writing to you, little children, because your sins are forgiven you for His name's sake" (1 John 2:12).

The Two Prophets in Revelation chapter 11 are God's men, and God will be using those Two Prophets to warn and prepare the world's people for Christ's Second Coming when He sets up His Millennial Kingdom on Earth. These Two Witnesses are there for the defense of the Gospel, but they are also witnesses for the prosecution (Romans 1-3). They usher in the beginning of God's Judgments on Mankind, and the Earth, just preceding Christ's Second Coming.

> *""He who believes in Him is not judged; he who does not believe has been judged already, because he has not believed in the name of the only begotten Son of God"* (John 3:18).

However, the judgments manifested by these Two Anointed Prophets are going to be mainly rejected, not only by unbelieversbut by many professing Christians as well. Plus, many of the now professing Christians will reject the Holiness Teachings and depart from the narrow way being presented by the Two Revelation Prophets. Thus, bringing about the Great Apostasy (the Departure from the Once for All Faith Delivered to The Saints.

Countless professing Christians (especially in the United States) think they are too good to go through any persecution or suffering. They do not understand that suffering and even death comes with the territory of being a Christian. The reality is that the world will hate the people of God without a cause. True Christians are lights to the world, and the darkness hates the lights because the lights expose their wickedness.

> *""Blessed are those who have been persecuted for the sake of righteousness, for theirs is the kingdom of heaven. "Blessed are you when men cast insults at you, and persecute you, and say all*

kinds of evil against you falsely, on account of Me.
"Rejoice and be glad, for your reward in heaven
is great, for so they persecuted the prophets who
were before you" (Matthew 5:10-12).

Yes, Jesus was loved by His Father, but He still had to
go to the cross for the greater good of all those who believe.
We must also understand that we are like sheep to led to the
slaughter (Romans 8:35-39), for the greater good of bringing
more people into the Kingdom. When the Church gets
persecuted, she will grow in numbers, and that is God's will.
It is like Tertullian said, "The blood of the martyrs is the seed
of the Church."

"And indeed, all who desire to live godly in
Christ Jesus will be persecuted" (2 Timothy 3:12).

You will be persecuted for telling people that their deeds
are evil, and they must repent of their sins and bring forth
fruit in keeping with that repentance.

"By no means let any of you suffer as a
murderer, or thief, or evildoer, or a troublesome
meddler; but if anyone suffers as a Christian, let
him not feel ashamed, but in that name let him
glorify God. For it is time for judgment to begin
with the household of God; and if it begins with us
first, what will be the outcome for those who do not
obey the gospel of God? And if it is with difficulty
that the righteous is saved, what will become of the
godless man and the sinner? Therefore, let those

also who suffer according to the will of God entrust their souls to a faithful Creator in doing what is right" (1 Peter 4:15- 19).

Remember when the apostles were flogged for preaching the gospel, they rejoiced for being worthy to suffer shame for His name. They knew the flogging was meant for Jesus, but since His critics could no longer get to Jesus, they persecuted His disciples. Moreover, the apostles took it as a badge of honor.

> *"But if it is of God, you will not be able to overthrow them; or else you may even be found fighting against God." And they took his advice; and after calling the apostles in, they flogged them and ordered them to speak no more in the name of Jesus, and then released them. So they went on their way from the presence of the council, rejoicing that they had been considered worthy to suffer shame for His name. And every day, in the temple and from house to house, they kept right on teaching and preaching Jesus as the Christ (Acts 5:39-42).*

Again, suffering as a Christian is a given because it comes with the territory. If you do not suffer as a Christian, you have to wonder if you are a legitimate Christian in the first place. If you get past the first question, then you have to wonder if you are living above reproach by living a Righteous and Holy Life. Then you have to evaluate if you are preaching the True

Gospel of The Lord Jesus Christ. Remember Paul said, "We should be followers of him as he was of Christ.

> *"But you followed my teaching, conduct, purpose, faith, patience, love, perseverance, persecutions, andsufferings, such as happened to me at Antioch, at Iconium and at Lystra; what persecutions I endured, and out of them all the Lord delivered me! And indeed, all who desire to live godly in Christ Jesus will be persecuted"* (2 Timothy 3:10-12).

The big question is who's on trial? However, the answer is not God? Neither God nor the Gospel (His Word) are on trial. Nevertheless, you are on trial if you are a member of the human race.

> *"Rather, let God be found true, though every man be found a liar, as it is written, "That Thou mightiest be justified in Thy words, and mightiest prevail when Thou art judged"* (Romans 3:4).

All of life's experiences and trials are a test to see if you have prepared yourself for living in the Kingdom of God and His Christ. So, the significant questions from His trials are this? What are you going to do with My Son the King, and what service are you going to render for Him? How are you going to fulfill God's will for your life?

> *"By grace you have been saved through faith; and that not of yourselves, it is the gift of God; not*

as a result of works, that no one should boast. For we are his workmanship, created in Christ Jesus for good works, which God prepared beforehand, that we should walk in them" (Ephesians 2:8-10).

Your words and your deeds will determine where you are going to spend eternity.

"The good man out of his good treasure brings forth what is good; and the evil man out of his evil treasure brings forth what is evil. "And I say to you, that every careless word that men shall speak, they shall render account for it in the day of judgment. "For by your words you shall be justified, and by your words you shall be condemned" (Matthew 12:35-37).

God's word says, *"All have sinned and fall short of the glory of God"* (**without exception**), and all of humanity will face God's judgments, so the question is this: What did you do with the Biblical Teachings of the Lord Jesus Christ? Your answer and your deeds will determine your eternal destiny, whether you are going to be declared innocent or guilty. You can believe or disbelieve God and His witnesses, and that is a matter of choice. However, the decision you make is not just choosing a Christian philosophy of life, but it is a matter of life and death, and that's how serious your decisions are in this matter.

"But thanks be to God, who always leads us in his triumph in Christ, and manifests through us

the sweetaroma of the knowledge of Him in every place. For we are a fragrance of Christ to God among those who are being saved and among those who are perishing; to the one an aroma from death to death, to the other an aroma from life to life. And who is adequate for these things? For we are not like many, peddling the word of God, but as from sincerity, but as from God, we speak in Christ in the sight of God" (2 Corinthians 2:14-17).

"Know this first of all, that in the last days mockers will come with their mocking, following after their own lusts, and saying, "Where is the promise of His coming? For ever since the Fathers fell asleep, all continues just as it was from the beginning of creation" (2 Peter 3:3-4).

Thus, there are doubters and mockers. They doubt God's word and mock because God has not destroyed them or the world yet! Their faulty thinking goes something like this, "I have not died of cancer yet, so it will not happen even in the future." They are naturalist and since God did not judge them yet, "They say it will never happen even in the future." Total foolishness! Peter then reminds them of God's judgments in the past with Noah's flood!

"For when they maintain this, it escapes their notice that by the word of God the heavens existed long ago and the earth was formed out of water and by water, through which the world at that

time was destroyed, being flooded with water. But the present heavens and earth by His word are being reserved for fire, kept for the day of judgment and destruction of ungodly men" (2 Peter 3:5-7).

These people should look around. The world is set up for destruction by fire. Fire from lightning, fire in the Earth (volcanoes), fire from above in the sun and fire from the stars (which includes meteors). The world does not have to worry about climate change, but they better start worrying about scorched Earth by fire. So, the question is, "Why is God delaying?"

"The Lord is not slow about His promise, as some count slowness, but is patient toward you, not wishing for any to perish but for all to come to repentance. But the day of the Lord will come like a thief, in which the heavens will pass away with a roar and the elements will be destroyed with intense heat, and the earth and its works will be burned up. Since all these things are to be destroyed in this way, what sort of people ought you to be in holy conduct and godliness, looking for and hastening the coming of the day of God, on account of which the heavens will be destroyed by burning, and the elements will melt with intense heat! But according to His promise we are looking for new heavens and a new earth, in which righteousness dwells" (2 Peter 3:9-13).

God is delaying because He wants all people to repent. They will have that opportunity now and during the first three and one-half years of the Tribulation to repent. That is during the preaching of the Two Prophets, but after their deaths, the Antichrist comes on the scene then shortly after that the Lord comes for His Saints (the Rapture of the Church). Then shortly after that, *"The Day of the Lord"* starts and then it will be virtually impossible to repent at that time. Why? Because the signs of the False Prophet and the Antichrist will be convincing and very deceiving. Their signs will be so compelling that even the elect will question what they are seeing and experiencing.

> *""For false Christs and false prophets will arise and will show great signs and wonders, so as to mislead, if possible, even the elect. "Behold, I have told you in advance"* (Matthew 24:24-25).

Plus, after the Rapture, there will be no human witnesses left because they would have been taken up in the Rapture.

> *""Then if anyone says to you, 'Behold, here is the Christ,' or 'There He is,' do not believe him. "For false Christs and false prophets will arise and will show great signs and wonders, so as to mislead, if possible, even the elect. "Behold, I have told you in advance. "If therefore they say to you, 'Behold, He is in the wilderness,' do not go forth, or, 'Behold, He is in the inner rooms,' do not believe them. "For just as the lightning comes from the east, and flashes even to the west, so shall*

the coming of the Son of Man be. "Wherever the corpse is, there the vultures will gather" (Matthew 24:23-28).

The false signs and wonders of the false prophets will be compelling, and they will try to convince you that they are God's spokesmen. However, Believers are to take special note of those people who follow the false teachers. Why? Because you will know them (false teachers) by the fruit they produce (the people who follow and support them), and where you find the spiritually dead people (unsaved), you will find the false teachers and false prophets(which are the vultures). They are also the religious wolves in sheep's clothing.

> *""Beware of the false prophets, who come to you in sheep's clothing, but inwardly are ravenous wolves. You will know them by their fruits. grapes are not gathered from thorn bushes, nor figs from thistles, are they? "Even so, every good tree bears good fruit; but the bad tree bears bad fruit"* (Matthew 7:15-17).

What is the fruit of the false prophets? Their followers and their sinful deeds. Check them out! Good trees (good teachers) bear good fruit, and bad trees (bad teachers) bear bad fruit. They both produce after their kind.

> *"And the kings of the earth and the great men and the commanders and the rich and the strong and every slave and free man, hid themselves in the caves and among the rocks of the mountains;*

*and they said to the mountains and to the rocks,
"Fall on us and hide us from the presence of Him
who sits on the throne, and from the wrath of the
Lamb; for the great day of their wrath has come;
and who is able to stand?"* (Revelation 6:15-17).

So, people must repent before the Day of Lord starts, and
that is why the Two Prophets come on the scene. God always
warns before He destroys and men better repent before they
experience the wrath of the Lamb.

*""And do not fear those who kill the body, but
are unable to kill the soul; but rather fear Him
who is able to destroy both soul and body in hell.
"Are not two sparrows sold for a cent? And yet not
one of them will fall to the ground apart from your
Father. "But the very hairs of your head are all
numbered. "Therefore do not fear; you are of more
value than many sparrows. "Everyone therefore
who shall confess Me before men, I will also confess
him before my Father who is in heaven. "But
whoever shall deny Me before men, I will also
deny him before My Father who is in heaven"*
(Matthew 10:28-33).

God's question to us is this? When the Great Day of the
Lamb's Wrath comes who can stand? The answer appears to
be very few. By this time the people of The Way would have
been caught up in the Rapture, and there will be no direct
witnesses (saved people) on the Earth to witness, so the Lord

along with His Heavenly Host of Angels will destroy those on the earth who failed to believe and repent.

> *"And the rest of mankind, who were not killed by these plagues, did not repent of the works of their hands, so as not to worship demons, and the idols of gold and of silver and of brass and of stone and of wood, which can neither see nor hear nor walk; and they did not repent of their murders nor of their sorceries nor of their immorality nor of their thefts"* (Revelation 9:20-21).

> *"But the day of the Lord will come like a thief, in which the heavens will pass away with a roar and the elements will be destroyed with intense heat, and the earth and its works will be burned up"* (2 Peter 3:10).

Why will He come like a thief? Because the people of the world did not listen to God's Prophets, and they will not listen to those Two Prophets who give mankind God's final warnings before destruction comes. They did not Wake Up, Listen Up, and they will Go Down. The Two Prophets will blow the trumpets to warn the people of the coming destruction. However, most of the world's people will fail to listen and get ready? Jesus said His coming would be like the days of Noah.

> *""For the coming of the Son of Man will be just like the days of Noah. "For as in those days which were before the flood they were eating*

and drinking, they were marrying and giving in marriage, until the day that Noah entered the ark, and they did not understand until the flood came and took them all away; so shall the coming of the Son of Man be" (Matthew 24:37-39).

They did not understand until it was too late. Right up to the time of the pending destruction, they were carrying on life as usual. They did not wake up or listen up because they continued to do the simple everyday things like eating and drinking, going to work and marrying and making plans for future marriages, etc. They did not get ready even after hearing the blasting trumpets.

That is the reason that God will send His Two Prophets, and the people of the world must listen to them. Many professing Christians believe that the Antichrist starts the Tribulation by signing a peace treaty with Israel (Daniel 9:24-27). However, it is not the Antichrist that confirms the covenant; it is the False Prophet. You cannot take the False Prophet lightly (he is the Wolf Pack Leader). If there is an inquisition type persecution, he will most likely be the one who heads it up (Revelation13:11ff). Remember the Antichrist only reigns for 42 months (three and one-half years), and we know that Antichrist's reign is in the last three and one-half years because he and the False Prophet will be thrown alive into the lake of fire.

"And the beast was seized, and with him the false prophet who performed the signs in his presence, by which he deceived those who had

received the mark of the beast and those who worshiped his image; these two were thrown alive into the lake of fire which burns with brimstone. And the rest were killed with the sword which came from the mouth of Him who sat upon the horse, and all the birds were filled with their flesh" (Revelation19:20-21).

The description of the Day *of the LORD* is simple. It is the period of time when The Lord Jesus Christ (God) leads His Angelic Hosts in the judgments of the world (its lands and its peoples). It is only at His Second Coming when He gets "directly" involved in the judgments.

God always wanted a man to rule over His Earthly creation, and Adam was that man. When Adam sinned, he forfeited his right to rule, and that rule was given to Satan. So, the Man Christ Jesus will come and set up His Kingdom on the Earth, and He will be King and Ruler over God's creation.

"These have the power to shut up the sky, in order that rain may not fall during the days of their prophesying; and they have power over the waters to turn them into blood, and to smite the earth with every plague, as often as they desire" (Revelation 11:6).

Yes, the beginning of the Tribulation starts with the Two Revelation Prophets bringing judgment upon the world. Thus, their coming is still an indirect judgment of God and does not initiate *The Day of the Lord,* but it does begin God's judgments in taking back control of His creation.

> *"Now we request you, brethren, with regard to the coming of our Lord Jesus Christ, and our gathering together to Him, that you not be quickly shaken from your composure or be disturbed either by a spirit or a message or a letter as if from us, to the effect that the day of the Lord has come. Let no one in any way deceive you, for it will not come unless the apostasy comes first, and the man of lawlessness is revealed, the son of destruction,"* (2 Thessalonians 2:1-3).

Paul is stating here that he knows when the Day of the Lord will start/come. He tells them that they do not need any more information about the date. He said, I already told you everything you need to know about His coming. Just be alert to the signs of the times. Many will say that Paul did not know when the Day of the Lord will start because not even Jesus knew?

> *""Truly I say to you, this generation will not pass away until all these things take place. "Heaven and earth will pass away, but my words shall not pass away. "But of that day and hour no one knows, not even the angels of heaven, nor the Son, but the Father alone"* (Matthew 24:34-37).

However, after His resurrection, Jesus knew.

"And so when they had come together, they were asking Him, saying, "Lord, is it at this time you are restoring the kingdom to Israel?" He said to them, "It is not for you to know times or epochs which the Father has fixed by His own authority; But you shall receive power when the Holy Spirit has come upon you; and you shall be My witnesses both in Jerusalem, and in all Judea and Samaria, and even to the remotest part of the earth." (Acts 1:6-8).

Jesus knew, but He did not tell the disciples at that time because they had more important things to do in spreading the gospel and that His coming would not come in their lifetime. Also, He didn't tell them about their persecutions at the beginning because they could not handle it before receiving the Spirit.

"These things I have spoken to you, that you may be kept from stumbling. "They will make you outcasts from the synagogue, but an hour is coming for everyone who kills you to think that he is offering service to God. "And these things they will do, because they have not known the Father, or Me. "But these things I have spoken to you, that when their hour comes, you may remember that I told you of them. and these things I did not say to you at the beginning, because I was with you. "But now I am going to Him who sent Me; and none of you asks Me, 'Where are You going?' "But

because I have said these things to you, sorrow has filled your heart" (John 16:1-7).

It is just like many today who cannot handle the idea of persecution because they are not truly saved, and if you are not indeed saved, you will not endure to the end. You will apostatize (depart from the True Biblical Faith).

> *""And the gospel must first be preached to all the nations. "And when they arrest you and deliver you up, do not be anxious beforehand about what you areto say, but say whatever is given you in that hour; for it is not you who speak, but it is the Holy Spirit. "And brother will deliver brother to death, and a father his child; and children will rise up against parents and have them put to death. "And you will be hated by all on account of My name, but the one who endures to the end, he shall be saved"* (Mark 13:10-13).

After His resurrection, Jesus knew the time that His Father fixed for all things, but He still did not tell his disciples.

> *"And so when they had come together, they were asking Him, saying, "Lord, is it at this time You are restoring the kingdom to Israel?" He said to them, "It is not for you to know times or epochs which the Father has fixed by His own authority; but you shall receive power when the Holy Spirit has come upon you; and you shall be My witnesses both in Jerusalem, and in all Judea and Samaria,*

and even to the remotest part of the earth" (Acts 1:6-8).

"But of that day and hour no one knows, not even the angels of heaven, nor the Son, but the Father alone" (Matthew 24:36).

Many error by misunderstanding this statement of Jesus of not knowing "The When" in the Gospel. The reason He did not know was simply that the Father did not tell Him "The When;" because neither He nor the disciples needed to know. They did not need to know because it was not going to happen in their lifetime. Jesus knew that He was not coming back for a long time, and to try and explain it to them would be way over their heads (John 16:12-13).

For the sons of Israel will remain for many days without king or prince, without sacrifice or sacred pillar, and without ephod or household idols. Afterward the sons of Israel will return and seek the LORD their God and David their king; and they will come trembling to the LORD and to His goodness in the last days (Hosea 3:4-5).

The most important thing that is often overlooked in this discussion is the fact that God's Revelation to us is progressive. Jesus knew after His resurrection and Paul came after Jesus. Just because Jesus did not know it while in the body does not mean that Paul did not know. Paul knew and was telling the Saints what signs would preceded the Rapture and the Day of the Lord.

> *"Now we request you, brethren, with regard to the coming of our Lord Jesus Christ, and our gathering together to Him, that you may not be quickly shaken from your composure or be disturbed either by a spirit or a message or a letter as if from us, to the effect that the day of the Lord has come. Let no one in any way deceive you, for it will not come **unless** the apostasy comes first, and the man of lawlessness is revealed, the son of destruction,"* (2 Thessalonians 2:1-3).

The first thing that has to be noted is the fact that here Paul is talking about two separate events. 1) One is the coming of the Lord for His Saints --- The Rapture. 2) The other event is "The Day of the Lord." However, the main emphasis of the passage is on "The Day of the Lord." Paul then tells the Thessalonian Church not to be deceived or disturbed by what they are experiencing (persecution), because the Day of the Lord has not come or started yet. Thus, putting the Rapture and the Day of the Lord close together, separated possibly only by days. So, the Rapture does happen just before the Day of the Lord starts. Yes, this is a Pre-Wrath Teaching. A good question at this point would be, "How long was Noah and the animals secure in the ark before it started to rain?"

> *"There went into the ark to Noah by twos, male and female, as God had commanded Noah. And it came about after the seven days, that the water of the flood came upon the earth"* (Genesis 7:9-10).

So, it appears that Noah, family, and animals were secure in the ark seven days before the water judgment came. This looks like a suitable picture/type of the Rapture and then the Day of the Lord. It appears that the seven-day separation between the Rapture and the Day of the Lord is a perfect time for the Marriage Supper of the Lamb. All the Saints would have been Raptured (no more witnesses on Earth) and those who have not been Raptured will experience the Divine Judgments of the Day of the Lord.

In those days a Jewish wedding lasted between five and seven days and our marriage supper to the Lamb will be a seven- day event. So, after the marriage supper, Jesus will start, "The Day of the Lord" judgments.

Again, the most challenging passage that the Pretribulation People have to deal with is this one referring to the Antichrist.

> *"And there was given to him a mouth speaking*
> *arrogant words and blasphemies; and authority*
> *to act for forty-two months was given to him"*
> (Revelation 13:5).

How long is he to act? Forty-two months (three and one-half years) and not seven years. This one verse destroys many of the Pretribulationists significant passages about the Antichrist. According to their interpretation of Daniel 9:27, they say, "The Antichrist" is going to start the Tribulation by signing a peace treaty with Israel for seven years. Impossible! He is not yet on the scene, and as such, a signing of a peace treaty with Israel would be considered **"an act!"**

185

""And he will make a firm covenant with the many for one week, but in the middle of the week he will put a stop to sacrifice and grain offering; and on the wing of abominations will come one who makes desolate, even until a complete destruction, one that is decreed, is poured out on the one who makes desolate" (Daniel 9:27).

The Lord Jesus Christ is the one that starts the Tribulation (and starts the Divine Clock) for Israel by opening the Seven Sealed Title Deed to the Earth.

"And they sang a new song, saying, "Worthy art Thou to take the book, and to break its seals; for Thou wast slain, and didst purchase for God with Thy blood men from every tribe and tongue and people and nation. "And Thou hast made them to be a kingdom and priests to our God; and they will reign upon the earth" (Revelation 5:9-10).

When the Divine Clock restarts for Israel's destiny, there are still seven years left on the Clock. However, within those seventy weeks of years, all of the following will have been accomplished.

""Seventy weeks have been decreed for your people and your holy city, to finish the transgression, to make an end of sin, to make atonement for iniquity, to bring in everlasting righteousness, to seal up vision and prophecy, and to anoint the most holy place" (Daniel 9:24).

The Two Revelation Prophets are going to be instrumental in fulfilling this prophecy that the Lord gave to Daniel. The Pretribulationists say, the Antichrist makes a Firm Covenant with the many for Seven Years (One Week), but if he only acts for 42 months, then the first part of this verse must be talking about the False Prophet and not the Antichrist.

> ""*And he* (the false prophet) *will make a firm covenant with the many for one week, but in the middle of the week he* (the false prophet) *will put a stop to sacrifice and grain offering; and on the wing of abominations will come one* (the Antichrist) *who makes desolate, even until a complete destruction, one that is decreed, is poured out on the one who makes desolate*" (Daniel 9:27).

The False Prophet and not the Antichrist will confirm the Mosaic Covenant (the Law). All he would have to do is confirm the Mosaic Covenant that already exists. There are several Abomination(s) that the Antichrist will carry out, but one of them that makes desolate is the forsaking or abandonment of the Mosaic Covenant. The Antichrist will eliminate the Mosaic Covenant by making it null and void. Thus, if anyone Jew or Gentile practices "ANY FORM" of Judaism or Christianity, they will be killed. He will demand total allegiance to himself. He will also overthrow (make desolate) the Roman Church that he used as a springboard for getting into power.

> ""*And the ten horns which you saw, and the beast, these will hate the harlot and will make her*

desolate and naked, and will eat her flesh and will burn her up with fire. "For God has put it in their hearts to executeHis purpose by having a common purpose, and by giving their kingdom to the beast, until the words of God should be fulfilled. "And the woman whom you saw is the great city, which reigns over the kings of the earth" (Revelation 17:16-18).

If the forsaking or abandonment of the Mosaic Covenant is an abomination to the Lord than today's false teachers, who say theydo not have to keep the Mosaic Law (falsely believing: "We are not under Law but under Grace") are also an abomination to the Lord.

"Not everyone who says to Me, 'Lord, Lord,' will enter the kingdom of heaven; but he who does the will of My Father who is in heaven. "Many will say to Me on that day, 'Lord, Lord, did we not prophesy in Your name, and in Your name cast out demons, and in Your name perform many miracles?' "And then I will declare to them, 'I never knew you; depart from Me, you who practice lawlessness" (Matthew 7:21- 23).

According to Matthew chapter 7, they practice lawlessness (sin), so they are not saved, but they are falsely teaching their people, "We are not under Law but under Grace." When one throws out the Law, it perverts the True Gospel, and they are presently doing what the Antichrist will eventually do (that is throwing out, making void the oracles of God). You are only under Grace if you are genuinely saved. These false teachers are truly not saved because they are still practicing lawlessness.

> *"Children, it is the last hour; and just as you heard that Antichrist is coming, even now many antichrists have arisen; from this we know that it is the last hour. They went out from us, but they were not really of us; for if they had been of us, they would have remained with us; but they went out, in order that it might be shown that they all are not of us. But you have an anointing from the Holy One, and you all know. I have not written to you because you do not know the truth, but because you do know it, and because no lie is of the truth"* (1 John 2:18-21).

The Scriptures teach that teachers who nullify the oracles of God (His Laws, statutes, and ordinances) are doing what the Antichrist will do in the future, that is nullifying God's Laws that were given to Moses. Thus, the false teachers are not only wolves in sheep's clothing but they are antichrists.

> *"For certain persons have crept in unnoticed, those who were long beforehand marked out for this condemnation, ungodly persons who turn the grace of our God into licentiousness* (disregarding accepted rules and standards) *and deny* (the finished work) *of our only Master and Lord, Jesus Christ (Jude 4).*

"Do not think that I came to abolish the Law or the Prophets; I did not come to abolish, but to fulfill. "For truly I say to you, until heaven and earth pass away, not the smallest letter or stroke shall pass away from the Law, until all is accomplished. "Whoever thenannuls one of the least of these commandments, andso teaches others, shall be called least in the kingdom of heaven; but whoever keeps and teaches them, he shall be called great in the kingdom ofheaven. "For I say to you, that unless your righteousness surpasses that of the scribes and Pharisees, you shall not enter the kingdom of heaven" (Matthew 5:17-20).

You are probably thinking that those false teachers will be offended by these teachings. Yes, and we say the same thing that Jesus said to the false teachers of His day.

"And after He called the multitude to Himself, He said to them, "Hear, and understand. "Not what enters into the mouth defiles the man, but what proceeds out of the mouth, this defiles the man." Then the disciples came and said to Him, "Do you know that the Pharisees were offended when they heard this statement?" But He answered and said, "Every plant which my heavenly Father did not plant shall be rooted up. "Let them alone; they are blind guides of the blind. and if a blind man guides a blind man, both will fall into a pit" (Matthew 15:10-14).

The main things that give these false teachers away is their lack of Law teachings (they are ashamed of the gospel) and they continue to make false assumptions that everyone they talk to is a Christian and a recipient of God's Grace. They assume everyone is a son of God, which is not the case. They do not say anything negative like, "You have to repent of your sin and bring forth fruit in keeping with that repentance." They tell their false sons about the good and beautiful things that God promises only to His True Sons.

> *For this is a rebellious people, false sons, sons who refuse to listen to the instruction of the LORD; Who say to the seers, "You must not see visions"; and to the prophets, "You must not prophesy to us what is right, speak to us pleasant words, prophesy illusions. "Get out of the way, turn aside from the path, let us hear no more about the Holy One of Israel." Therefore thus says the Holy One of Israel, "Since you have rejected this word, and have put your trust in oppression and guile, and have relied on them, therefore this iniquity will be to you like a breach about to fall, a bulge in a high wall, whose collapse comes suddenly in an instant. "And whose collapse is like the smashing of a potter's jar; soruthlessly shattered that a sherd will not be found among its pieces to take fire from a hearth, or to scoop water from a cistern"* (Isaiah 30:9-14).

So, false teachers give what their false sons want. The false sons want to hear lies, and the false teachers accommodate their wishes.

> ""Wherever the corpse is, there thevultures will gather" (Matthew 24:28).

> "For thus the Lord God, the Holy One of Israel,has said, "In repentance and rest you shall be saved,in quietness and trust is your strength." But you were not willing," (Isaiah 30:15).

They were unwilling to repent and be saved. So, are you a true son who listens or a false son who refuses to listen? Again, neither the False Prophet nor the Antichrist starts the Tribulation; God does. So, the people of The Way should be looking for the Two Prophets coming on the scene and not be looking for the Rapture or the Antichrist. We know that the world's people (will be looking out) and not be looking for the Two Prophets, because they know they will get an earful. Their ears will not be tickled but their ears will get a good ringing.

> "He who has an ear, let him hear what the Spirit says to the churches. He who overcomes shall not be hurt by the second death" (Revelation 2:11).

> "Let no one in any way deceive you, for it will not come unless the apostasy comes first, and the man of lawlessness is revealed, the son of destruction, who opposes and exalts himself above

every so- called god or object of worship, so that he takes his seat in the temple of God, displaying himself as being God. Do you not remember that while I was still with you, I was telling you these things?" (2 Thessalonians 2:3-5).

What will not come? *"The Day of the Lord."* The Day of the Lord will not come unless the apostasy (The Great Falling Away) comes first. Again, God starts the Divine Clock for the seven-year Tribulation period when he breaks the first seal.

"For the mystery of lawlessness is already at work; only he who now restrains will do so until he is taken out of the way. And then that lawless one will be revealed whom the Lord will slay with the breath of His mouth and bring to an end by the appearance of His coming; that is, the one whose coming is in accord with the activity of Satan, with all power and signs and false wonders, and with all the deception of wickedness for those who perish, because they did not receive the love of the truth so as to be saved. And for this reason God will send upon them a deluding influence so that they might believe what is false, in order that they all may be judged who did notbelieve the truth, but took pleasure in wickedness" (2 Thessalonians 2:7-12).

Yes, the mystery of lawlessness is already at work, even now the works of the Devil are in the world because he is the god of this world and his lawless teachers and lawless people follow him in his rebellion against God. The Holy Spirit is presently restraining Satan and the Antichrist from coming on the scene until He determines the time. Then, when the time is right at the midway point of the Tribulation, the Holy Spirit will lift His restraining power, and all hell will break loose from heaven and come to the Earth.

> *"Now the salvation, and the power, and the kingdom of our God and the authority of His Christ have come, for the accuser of our brethren* (the Devil)*has been thrown down, who accuses them before our God day and night. "And they* (The people of The Way) *overcame him because of the blood of the Lamb and because of the word of their testimony, and they did not love their life even to death. "For this reason, rejoice, O heavens and you who dwell in them. Woe to the earth and the sea, because the devil has come down to you, having great wrath, knowing that he has only a short time"* (Revelation 12:10-12).

It is true that all of the riders on the horses are God's judgments. God will answer the prayers of His Prophets and they along with The Spirit of God will prepare His sheep for the Lord's Second Coming. But it is God who is in charge of both His Prophets and His People. Remember the Antichrist acts only for forty-two months, and they will be the last 42 months. God does not want you to be deceived.

> *Let no one in any way deceive you, for it will not come unless the apostasy comes first, and the man*

of lawlessness is revealed, the son of destruction, who opposes and exalts himself above every so-called god or object of worship, so that he takes his seat in the temple of God, displaying himself as being God. Do you not remember that while I was still with you, I was telling you these things?" (2 Thessalonians 2:3-5).

What will not come? *The Day of the Lord* will not come unless the apostasy (the falling away) comes first. So, do not be surprised when the massive exodus comes. Why not? Because it is written in the Scriptures, but it is the True Gospel Preaching of the Two Prophets that will further bring about (or even solidify) the Apostates departure and not the Antichrist.

The Antichrist is not yet on the scene when the massive apostasy takes place. The professing Christians will fail to believe in present-day sanctification because they know they cannot stop sinning. You cannot and must not judge by appearances (John 7:24), you must judge righteously because numbers on one side or the other are irrelevant.

"Do not judge according to appearance, but judge with righteous judgment" (John 7:24).

Many are following the broad road to destruction, and yes, more people are going to hell than those who are going to heaven!

"Enter by the narrow gate; for the gate is wide, and the way is broad that leads to destruction, and many are those who enter by it. "For the gate is small, and the way is narrow that leads to life, andfew are those who find it" (Matthew 7:13-14).

Several other factors will cause the apostasy. We already noted that many will fall away because they love the world, many willfall away because of persecution and false teachers, and others do not have a clue as to what is going on, they do not know God nor dothey understand His ways. Others are immature, and they cannot even tell the difference between good and evil, right and wrong, and God and the Devil. Then there are the Two Prophets who preach Repentance and Holy Living (to stop sinning). Added to that is the erroneous preaching of the Pretribulation Rapture Theorist.

Why are the Pretribulation Rapture Teachers a factor? Because these prophecy preachers are presently telling their peopleof the certainty of the Pretribulation Rapture. However, when it does not happen, their followers will question their gospel message and even wonder if there will be a Rapture. They will say, "You were so sure of your Pretribulation Teachings that we believed you and we did not prepare or get ready for what is presently happening. You told us we would not be here, and that teaching put us to sleep. Yes, we are guilty because we did not thoroughly check it out for ourselves, but hopefully most of us are now awake and listening.

According to Matthew chapter 24, the next thing that Jesus said would happen is the persecution of the Saints. Many of the Saints will be killed, and some even before the Antichrist comes on the scene. The world's people will hate those Two Revelation 11 Prophets because of their judgments on the Earth and their Teachings of a Strict Adherence to the Law, Grace, and Holy Living. The world's people will love to kill them (to silence them) and persecute anyone who follows their Holiness Teachings as found in the Scriptures.

The only reason that the people of The Way are not physically persecuted at this present time in the United States is due to the watered-down gospel message, and the people of the world have no discernment as to our true numbers and our true identity. The world's people think all who say they are Christians are disciples; they are clueless!

> *"See how great a love the Father has bestowed upon us, that we should be called children of God; and such we are. For this reason the world does not know us, because it did not know Him"* (1 John 3:1).

The more Christians there are, the safer you are. God told Paul he was safe in the city of Corinth because He had many believers in that city.

> *"And Crispus, the leader of the synagogue, believed in the Lord with all his household, and many of the Corinthians when they heard were believing and being baptized. And the Lord said*

to Paul in the night by a vision, "Do not be afraid any longer, but goon speaking and do not be silent; for I am with you, and no man will attack you in order to harm you, for I have many people in this city. "And he settled therea year and six months, teaching the word of God among them" (Acts 18:8-11).

That is why the people of The Way should evangelize now, because we have at least perceived numbers, but when the apostasy is in full bloom the world's people will see how few we are in number and persecutions will increase.

""Then they will deliver you to tribulation, and will kill you, and you will be hated by all nations on account of My name. "And at that time many will fall away and will deliver up one another and hate one another. "And many false prophets will arise, and willmislead many. "And because lawlessness is increased, most people's love will grow cold. "But the one who endures to the end, he shall be saved. "Andthis gospel of the kingdom shall be preached in the whole world for a witness to all the nations, and then the end shall come" (Matthew 24:9-14).

The true people of The Way cannot and will not depart because they have the Spirit of the Living God in them, and God promises and guarantees our success. Not the success of avoiding persecution or even death, but the success of future glory and rewards.

""Now at that time Michael, the great prince who stands guard over the sons of your people, will arise. and there will be a time of distress such as never occurred since there was a nation until that time; and at that time your people, everyone who is found written in the book, will be rescued. "And many of those who sleep in the dust of the ground will awake, these to everlasting life, but the others to disgrace and everlasting contempt." And those who have insight will shine brightly like the brightness of the expanse of heaven, and those who lead the many to righteousness, like the stars forever and ever. "But as for you, Daniel, conceal these words and seal up the book until the end of time; many will go back and forth, and knowledge will increase" (Daniel 12:1-4).

We ought always to give thanks to God for you, brethren, as is only fitting, because your faith is greatly enlarged, and the love of each one of you toward one another grows ever greater; therefore, we ourselves speak proudly of you among the churches of God for your perseverance and faith in the midst of all your persecutions and afflictions which you endure. This is a plain indication of God's righteous judgment so that you may be considered worthy of the kingdom of God, for which indeed you are suffering. For after all it is only just for God to repay with affliction those who afflict you, and to give relief to you who are afflicted and to us as well when the Lord Jesus shall be revealed from heaven with His mighty angels in flaming fire, dealing out retribution to those who do not know God and to those who do not obey the gospel of our Lord Jesus. And these will pay the penalty of eternal destruction, away from the presence of the Lord and from the glory of His power,when He comes to be glorified in His saints on that day, and to be marveled at among all who have believed-- for our testimony to you was believed. To this end also we pray for you always that our God may count you worthy of your calling, and fulfill every desire for goodness and the work of faith with power; in order that the name of our Lord Jesus may be glorified in you, and you in Him, according to the grace of our God and the Lord Jesus Christ" (2 Thessalonians 1:3-12).

Throughout history, many of the Saints have wondered how the gospel of the Kingdom would be preached to the whole world?

""But the one who endures to the end, he shall be saved. "This gospel of the kingdom shall be preached in the whole world for a witness to all the nations, and then the end shall come" (Matthew 24:13-14).

Even when we were sending out missionaries, we knew it was a daunting task. The answer can be found in the attention-getting trumpet blasts (signs) of the Two Prophets. They will get some ofthe world's attention with the signs, and the world will be able to see their dead bodies in Jerusalem via television and the internet. However, like in the days of Noah; the vast majority of people will be carrying on life as usual, but those days will be anything but "as usual." (Matthew 16:1-4).

> *""And just as it happened in the days of Noah, so it shall be also in the days of the Son of Man: they were eating, they were drinking, they were marrying, they were being given in marriage, until the day that Noah entered the ark, and the flood came and destroyed them all. "It was the same as happened in the days of lot: they were eating, they were drinking, they were buying, they were selling, they were planting, they were building; but on the day that lot went out from Sodom it rained fire and brimstone from heaven and destroyed them all. "It will be just the same on the day that the Son of Man is revealed"* (Luke 17:26-30).

The people of The Way will be in the Tribulation, and many will be killed (but not all), and all nations will hate them because of His Name. Again, they will even try to kill those Two Prophets, but God will protect them until their ministry is completed after three and one- half years. The same is true for all the people of The Way; you will not die until your work on Earth is done. We are to walk in the works that He prepared for us to walk in and we will be the victors.

"And we know that God causes all things to work together for good to those who love God, to those who are called according to His purpose. For whom He foreknew, He also predestined to become conformed to the image of His Son, that He might be the first-born among many brethren; and whom He predestined, these He also called; and whom He called, these He also justified; and whom He justified, these He also glorified" (Romans 8:28-30).

If you are the predestined, then you are the called, and if you are the called, you are also justified, and if you are justified, you are also the glorified. Look forward to the future joy! Jesus looked forward to it, and that is why He was able to endure to the end.

"Therefore, since we have so great a cloud of witnesses surrounding us, let us also lay aside every encumbrance, and the sin which so easily entangles us, and let us run with endurance the race that is set before us, fixing our eyes on Jesus, the author and perfecter of faith, who for the joy set before Him endured the cross, despising the shame, and has sat down at the right hand of the throne of God. For consider Him who has endured such hostility by sinners against Himself, so that you may not grow weary and lose heart. You have not yet resisted to the point of shedding blood in your striving against sin; And you have forgotten

*the exhortation which is addressed to you as sons,
"My son, do not regard lightly the discipline of the
Lord, nor faint when you are reproved by Him; for
those whom the Lord loves He disciplines, and He
scourges every son whom He receives"* (Hebrews
12:1-6).

Be reminded that nothing can happen to you without
your Father's permission. You are more valuable than many
sparrows (Matthew 10:29-33).

*"And I will grant authority to My two witnesses,
and they will prophesy for twelve hundred and
sixty days, clothed in sackcloth." These are the two
olive trees and the two lampstands that stand
beforethe Lord of the earth. And if anyone desires
to harm them, fire proceeds out of their mouth and
devours their enemies; and if anyone would desire
to harm them, in this manner he must be killed*
(Revelations 11:3- 5).

People may even doubt if those Two Prophets are legitimate.
They will say something foolish like, "Literal Fire" is not
coming out of their mouths, and they are not the reincarnated
prophets that God promised, etc. However, fire in the Bible
represents judgment (e.g., Hell's Fire). Those Two Prophets
will be able to kill those who are trying to kill them with fiery
judgment words from their mouths. The false teachers will
also say something like what they said to Jesus.

"Did not Moses give you the Law, and yet none of you carries out the Law? Why do you seek to kill Me?" The multitude answered, "You have a demon! Who seeks to kill you?" (John 7:19-20).

"If they called the head of our household the Devil, what do you think they will call you?

"A disciple is not above his teacher, nor a slave above his master. "It is enough for the disciple that he become as his teacher, and the slave as his master. If they have called the head of the house Beelzebub, how much more the members of his household! "Therefore do not fear them, for there is nothing covered that will not be revealed, and hidden that will not be known. "What I tell you in the darkness, speak in the light; and what you hear whispered in your ear, proclaim upon the housetops (Matthew 10:24-27).

The Day of the Lord will not come until after these Two Prophets are killed. Then when, "The Day of the Lord" comes the Lord will take vengeance on all those who killed His Prophets and His witnesses. When Paul was persecuting the Church, Jesus asked Paul (formerly Saul), "Why are you persecuting Me"?

"Now Saul, still breathing threats and murder against the disciples of the Lord, went to the high priest, and asked for letters from him to the synagogues at Damascus, so that if he found any

belonging to the Way, both men and women, he might bring them bound to Jerusalem. And it came about that as he journeyed, he was approaching Damascus, and suddenly a light from heaven flashedaround him; and he fell to the ground, and heard a voice saying to him, "Saul, Saul, why are you persecuting Me?" And he said, "Who art Thou, Lord?" and he said, "I am Jesus whom you are persecuting" (Acts 9:1-5).

When you persecute God's children/people, you are persecuting Christ. The people of God are part of His Body, and He will not let those who persecuted His Church (His Body) go unpunished. Thus, *the Day of the Lord* will be the Lord's vengeance. However, take special note that the killing of God's people (Saints) is not God's wrath, but evil men are doing the deeds of their father, the Devil, who was a murderer from the beginning (John 8:44-47). Remember that it is Satan using fallen men and fallen angels against God's and against the Redeemed Children of God (Spiritual Warfare).

Being killed as a martyr appears to be physical warfare, but this is often the form that Spiritual Warfare takes. Spiritual Warfare is for the souls of men and Satan will lie, scheme, and even kill to keep men from knowing the truth about God and His plan for man's salvation.

"Finally, be strong in the Lord, and in the strength of His might. Put on the full armor of God, that you may be able to stand firm against the schemes of the devil. For our struggle is not

against flesh and blood, but against the rulers, against the powers, against the world forces of this darkness, against the spiritual forces of wickedness in the heavenly places. Therefore, take up the full armor of God, that you may be able to resist in the evil day, and having doneeverything, to stand firm" (Ephesians 6:10-13).

Matthew chapter 24, Revelation 6 and 11 are comparative passages of Scripture that most Prophetic Teachers look too. They compare Matthew chapter 24 and Revelation chapter 6 and conclude that the Antichrist (is the Rider on the White Horse) that starts the Tribulation. Their misunderstanding of Daniel 9:24-27 supports this belief.

The first and most important thing about the Pretribulation Rapture Theory is that it is only a theory and a theory that is not onlyimprobable but impossible. Why impossible? Because we previouslyread in 2 Thessalonians 2:3-5, Malachi 4:5 and Acts 2:17-20 of six significant events that have to occur **before** the Day of the Lord starts:

1. His Two Witnesses (**JAMES and U R2 JOHN**) come on thescene.
2. There is the Increased Apostasy.
3. The Antichrist is revealed to the world by the Two Witnesses.
4. The Temple has to be built for the Lord's Coming, and it will also be used for the introduction of the Antichrist as he carries out THE ABOMINATION OF DESOLATION.

5. The Sign Gift of Languages (Tongues) are re-instituted.
6. Then there are the Cosmic Disturbances.

All these things must happen before the Day of the Lord starts. Paul wrote his letter to the Church at Thessalonica, informing them that they were not in the Day of the Lord. They were experiencing severe persecution, but again, Paul reminded them that certain things had to happen before the Day of the Lord starts.

The Book of the Revelation is the Revelation of the Lord Jesus Christ and not the Revelation of Satan. However, there will be the revealing of the Antichrist by the Two Prophets. They will give you his name and the calculation number adding up to 666 at the beginning of their ministry. Thus, the world will have to wait some 3½ years to see if their prophecy and the identity of the Antichrist comes to pass. However, the False Prophet's identity will be known almost immediately.

*"Here is wisdom. let him who has understanding
calculate the number of the beast, for the number
is that of a man; and his number is six hundred
and sixty-six"* (Revelation 13:17-18).

However, be warned, these Two Prophets are *Judgment Prophets* that are from God. They will be the first on the scene to call the world to repentance, and they will call all Israelites home and God will whistle (Zechariah10:8-10) for all Jews to come home (Aliyah).

The Two Prophets will tell the world who the Antichrist is and that God's Time Clock for the Seven Years of Tribulation (Daniel 9:24-27) has officially started. The Two Prophets will immediately close up the sky, and it will not rain worldwide for the length of their ministry (3½ years). During that time the Temple will be rebuilt.

Thus, the critical question is this: "When does the Day *of the Lord* commence? The answer is after the six previously mentioned events take place. The Pretribulation People give a definition to the Day *of the Lord that fits* their theology, but that definition does not agree with the teachings in the Word of God. Their general description of the Day of the Lord is that the Tribulation (a sevenyear period) is another name for the Day of the Lord.

However, the purpose of the Two Witnesses of Revelation 11 is to get people saved during the Tribulation by preaching, "The Faith that was Once for All Delivered to the Saints." Their Gospel Message will not change from the Original Gospel. People will continue to be Saved by Faith and Sealed by the Holy Spirit. Remember, these Two Prophets are not bringing a new Revelation; they are reiterating and carrying out the already existing writings of the Old and New Testaments.

Ultimately, the New Covenant is a promise from God to Israel (Jeremiah 31:31-34), and they will receive the promise. The following verses are telling us what God will do during the Tribulationto Israel and the Gentile nations.

*17 "AND IT SHALL BE IN THE LAST DAYS,' God says, 'THAT I WILL POUR FORTH OF MY SPIRIT UPON ALL MANKIND; AND YOUR SONS AND YOUR DAUGHTERS SHALL PROPHESY, AND AND YOUR YOUNG MEN SHALL SEE VISIONS, AND YOUR OLD MEN SHALL DREAM DREAMS; 18 EVEN UPON MY BONDSLAVES, BOTH MEN AND WOMEN, I WILL IN THOSE DAYS POUR FORTH OF MY SPIRIT AND THEY SHALL PROPHESY. 19 'AND I WILL GRANT WONDERS IN THE SKY ABOVE, AND SIGNS ON THE EARTH BENEATH, BLOOD, AND FIRE, AND VAPOR OF SMOKE. 20 'THE SUN SHALL BE TURNED INTO DARKNESS, AND, AND THE MOON INTO BLOOD, **BEFORE** THE GREAT AND GLORIOUS DAY OF THE LORD SHALL COME. 'AND IT SHALL BE, THAT EVERYONE WHO CALLS ON THE NAME OF THE LORD SHALL BE SAVED'* (Acts 2:17-21).

The Day of the Lord cannot be synonymous with the Tribulation because the Tribulation events happen between verses 17 and 20b. Then in 20c, we see that these Tribulation events will come **before** the Great and Glorious Day of the Lord. All the events mentioned in Acts chapter 2 did not happen at the first Pentecost, but they will occur in the last days.

The problem with the Pretribulation Rapture Theorist is that no one can be saved during the Tribulation because then they would have missed the Rapture, and will have to go through The Wrath of God. Their teachings on the Rapture is the same as other cults. How is that? They would say, "If you come under our umbrella of teachings, you will escape the judgments of God."

> *"Alas, you who are longing for the day of the LORD, for what purpose will the day of the LORD be to you? It will be darkness and not light; as when a man flees from a lion, and a bear meets him, or goes home, leans his hand against the wall, and a snake bites him. Will not the day of the LORD be darkness instead of light, even gloom with no brightness in it?"* (Amos 5:18-20).

There is no brightness when the Day of the Lord starts. Thus, the Rapture (seven days earlier) is a "Day of Light," whereas the Day of the Lord is darkness and there is no brightness in it!.

> *"But you, brethren, are not in darkness, that the day should overtake you like a thief; for you are all sons of light and sons of day. We are not of night nor of darkness; so then let us not sleep as others do, but let us be alert and sober. For those who sleep do their sleeping at night, and those who get drunk get drunk at night. But since we are of the day, let us be sober, having put on the breastplate of faith*

and love, and as a helmet, the hope of salvation"
(1 Thessalonians 5:4-8).

Yes, the Pretribulationists rightly believe that the Rapture will precede the Day of the Lord. However, the Day of the Lord does not begin at the beginning of the Tribulation. None of the things mentioned in Amos happens during the first 3½ years of the Tribulation when the Two Prophets are on the scene. So, the Rapture will take place just before the Day of the Lord starts.

The True People of God do not have to worry about the Wrathof the Day of the Lord, because they would have been taken out the week before the Day of the Lord starts.

#14 REVELATION CHAPTER 6
THE FOUR HOUSEMEN

The Day of the Lord does not start at the beginning of the Tribulation. *The Day of the Lord* does not even commence with the opening of the seals. The first seal has a Rider on a White Horse. He rides the leading horse and the White Horse carries the Victory Rider. The Rider on the White Horse is the Prophet like Moses and like The Lord Jesus Christ (**JAMES**). The White Horse is the Victor's Horse, and the rest of the horses and their riders follow his leading. The White Horse Rider gives us God's final warnings before the coming Day of the Lord.

> *"And the LORD utters His voice before His army; surely His camp is very great, for strong is He who carries out His word. The day of the Lord is indeed great and very awesome, and who can endure it?"* Joel 2:11 (simple verse about the day of the LORD).

The Day of the Lord is when God and His army of angels bring destruction on man, Satan, and the lands. Thus, it does not appear that many people will be able to stand during the Day of the Lord, except the Jews who escaped to the wilderness (which includes the 144,000) when they eventually look up in faith and get redeemed.

THE FIRST SEAL

In Revelation chapter 6, most professing Christians believe that the Rider on the White Horse is the Antichrist. As such, they do not have the discernment to know who is doing what; and why?

> *"And I saw when the Lamb broke one of the seven seals, and I heard one of the four living creatures saying as with a voice of thunder, "Come." (Permission to Go). And I looked, and behold, a white horse, and he who sat on it had a bow; and a crown was given to him; and he went out conquering, and to conquer"* (Revelation 6:1-2).

Later in the Book of the Revelation, Jesus Christ is the Victory Rider on the White Horse. So, many of these prophecy teachers, at one time say the rider on the Victory White Horse is the Antichrist and the other time it is The Lord Jesus Christ. This teaching creates a significant problem for them, even if they do not realize it.

> *"And I saw heaven opened; and behold, a white horse, and He who sat upon it is called Faithful and True; and in righteousness He judges and*

ROBERT "BOB" DOBRANSKI, MDiv

wageswar" (Revelations 19:11 Here Jesus Christ
is the White Horse Victory Rider).

The Victors ride the White Horses. The White Horse
Rider of Revelation 6:1-2 is the fulfillment of "The Prophet"
or "That Prophet" (**JAMES**). He will act as Israel's deliver.
The bow he carries is a signof strength and might (Jeremiah
49:35 and Hosea 1:5). He does not have the arrows of warfare,
because his battles are with the SpiritualForces of Wickedness
in the Heavenly Places.

> *"And I saw when the Lamb broke one of the
> seven seals, and I heard one of the four living
> creatures saying as with a voice of thunder,
> "Come." And I looked, and behold, a white horse,
> and he who sat on it had a bow; and a crown was
> given to him; and he went out conquering, and to
> conquer"* (Revelation 6:1-2).

To conquer, nikao (nik-ah'-o); means to subdue (literally or
figuratively): "to overcome" (its usual meaning), is translated
"conquering" and "to conquer" KJV - conquer, overcome,
prevail, get the victory. (Vine's Expository Dictionary of
Biblical Words)

The first and most important thing to note is that God
would never identify the Antichrist as an overcomer, one who
prevails or a victor.

The White Horse Rider is a Victor—a Winner. Remember
he represents the Church(es); he is one of the Lampstands

(Revelation 1:20 and Revelation 11:4). Also, be reminded what Jesus said, "I will build My Church and the Gates of Hades shall not overpower it! (Matthew 16:18).

> *"He who has an ear, let him hear what the Spirit says to the churches. He who overcomes shall not be hurt by the second death"* (Revelation 2:11).

> *"But in all these things we overwhelmingly conquer through Him who loved us* (Romans 8:37).

All of God's people are conquerors and victors. Yes, you should be able to give a defense for what you believe to everyone who asks of you, including the inquisitor. However, when the inquisitor asks you, "Are you one of those witnesses for The Lord Jesus Christ who is preaching repentance from sin and throwing ourcities into confusion?" You can answer in the affirmative.

> *""I have given them Thy word; and the world has hated them, because they are not of the world, even as I am not of the world"* (John 17:14 Jesus said).

All of God's people will be victorious like Jesus, and "The Prophet" like Moses (JAMES) will also be victorious. All of God's people will be victorious in their spiritual battles against the schemesof the Devil. No, they will not use guns and arrows to win the victory,they will use the Sword of the

Spirit, which is the Word of God (see Paul as a victor in 1 Corinthians 9:23-27).

> "Then he answered and said to me, "This is the word of the LORD to Zerubbabel saying, 'Not by might nor by power, but by My Spirit,' says the LORD of hosts" (Zechariah 4:6).

All of God's people have the Sword of the Spirit, and they mustpractice and know how to use it most effectively (also see Ephesians 6:11-20). So, the Lord Jesus Christ (God) is starting the Tribulation by opening the seals and sending the White Horse Rider in His stead. This rider had a bow which pictures strength and might,but he will be a diplomat. He will convince Israel's leadership (a Zerubbabel type individual) that it is time to rebuild the Temple. Yes,it will lead to war (the Red Horse Rider follows the White Horse), but these Two Revelation Prophets do not conquer by force, but by the Spirit of God.

> *"Then he answered and said to me, "This is the word of the LORD to Zerubbabel saying, 'Not by might nor by power, but by My Spirit,' says the LORD of hosts"* (Zechariah 4:6).

He (JAMES) conquers and wins the victory by doing God's will and gets the Victory over lost souls by preaching the Word, and he tells the people of The Way how they can get the victory over sin and Satan. God will do this by pouring out His Spirit upon all of humanity who believes and receives The Lord Jesus Christ (Acts 2:16-21).

"For though we walk in the flesh, we do not war according to the flesh, for the weapons of our warfare are not of the flesh, but divinely powerful for the destruction of fortresses. We are destroying speculations and every lofty thing raised up against the knowledge of God, and we are taking every thought captive to the obedience of Christ, and we are ready to punish all disobedience, whenever your obedience is complete" (2 Corinthians10:3-7).

So, what kind of Crown was given to him (JAMES)?

"And I looked, and behold, a white horse, and he who sat on it had a bow; and a crown was given to him; and he went out conquering, and to conquer" (Revelation 6:2).

It is the Victor's Crown, but take special note that the Crown was "given to him"–and not taken. This indicates a Third Person (The Lord Jesus Christ) is giving His authority, to the White Horse Rider, to act in His stead and to accomplish His work. So, what does one have to do to get the Victor's Crown? Do what Paul told Timothy to do:

"You then, my son, be strong in the grace that is in Christ Jesus. And the things you have heard me say in the presence of many witnesses entrust to reliable men who will also be qualified to teach others. Endure hardship with us like a good soldier of Christ Jesus. No one serving as a soldier gets involved in civilian affairs, so that he wants

to please his commanding officer. Similarly, if anyone competes as an athlete, he does not receive the victor's crown unless he competes according to the rules. The hardworking farmer should be the first to receive a share of the crops. Reflect on what I am saying, for the Lord will give you insight into all this" (2 Timothy 2:1-7 NIV).

We see that for one to receive the Victor's Crown, one must be a Teacher of Teachers. He must be one who can endure hardship like a Good Soldier and who is in full-time ministry (like a Good Soldier). He is one who wants to please God (His Commander) in whatever he does, and one does not receive the Victor's Crown unless he competes according to the rules. He cannot be one who does his own thing; he must carry out the will of God. He must know the Rule Book (the Bible) and stay within the Rules of Engagement given to him by God. Verse 7 that follows verse 6 of 2 Timothy 2 (quoted above) is definitely worth noting.

"Reflect on what I am saying, for the Lord will give you insight into all this" (2 Timothy 2:7 NIV).

It is obvious that not all of God's people will receive the Victor's Crown, but do you want insight on something really great? We said that the White Horse Riders are the Victory Riders! Amen! When the Lord returns to Earth on His White Victory Horse, guess what color horses the Saints are riding? You got it! All the Saints will be riding, "White Horses of Victory!"

*And He is clothed with a robe dipped in blood;
and His name is called The Word of God. And the
armies which are in heaven, clothed in fine linen,
white and clean, were following Him on white
horses* (Revelation 19:13-14).

Many say, "The White Horse Rider is the Antichrist"
and there are no arrows; thus, he wins over by diplomacy.
However, what kind of diplomatic victory is it if the next
thing that follows is war? Not a very good antiwar diplomat.
So, who is the Rider on the White Horse? Alternatively, more
significantly, who are some of the Riders on the Various
Colored Horses? The First White Horse Rider is God's
Prophet (JAMES). The next three horses are demonic forces
that carry out the judgments of the Leading White Horse
Rider.

*"Then the LORD said to Moses, "See, I make
you as God to Pharaoh, and your brother Aaron
shall be your prophet. You shall speak all that I
command you, and your brother Aaron shall speak
to Pharaoh that he let the sons of Israel go out of
his land"*(Exodus 7:1-2).

The Lord is making that Prophet, JAMES, as God
not only to one King --- Pharaoh, but to all The Nation's
Leaders (Secular and Religious). These World Leaders should
follow the example of the King and people of Nineveh at
the preaching of Jonah (Jonah 3:1- 10). Moreover, just like
Aaron was Moses Prophet, U R2 JOHN will be the Prophet
of JAMES. So, if anyone even tries to attack the Prophets,

they are not attacking them, but their teachings, which were given to them by God.

> *"And there was given me a measuring rod like a staff; and someone said* (probably JAMES), *"Rise and measure the temple of God, and the altar, and those who worship in it. "And leave out the court which is outside the temple, and do not measure it, for it has been given to the nations; and they will tread underfoot the holy city for forty-two months"*(Revelation 11:1-2).

A measuring rod like a staff was given to U R2 JOHN. He is to measure the Temple and the Altar and the people who worship in it. It appears that the measuring comes after the Temple, and the Altar have been built? U R2 JOHN does not have to measure the outer court because that has been given to the Gentile Nations. U R2 JOHN was given the measuring rod and the Two Revelation Prophets will make sure the Temple is completed before their departure. Yes, the building of the Temple will start a war and even ultra-skeptics would agree with that scenario.

THE SECOND SEAL

> *"And when He broke the second seal, I heard the second living creature saying, "Come" (*Permission to Go). *And another, a red horse, went out; and to him who sat on it, it was granted to take peace from the earth, and that men should slay one*

another; and a great sword was given to him"
(Revelation 6:3-4).

Yes, the Two Revelation Prophets will cause peace to be taken from the Earth. They will see that the Temple gets built, they will stop the rain that results in drought and famine conditions, and professing Christian family members will be against their own family members because of the Unadulterated Gospel Message,.

> *"Do you suppose that I came to grant peace on earth? I tell you, no, but rather division; for from now on five members in one household will be divided, three against two, and two against three. "They will be divided, father against son, and son against father; mother against daughter, and daughter against mother; mother-in-law against daughter-in- law, and daughter-in-law against mother-in-law"* (Luke 12:51-53).

"U R2 JOHN" will also have the Sword of the Spirit. It will function like a two-edged sword with one side being like a scalpel that heals (he will restore the hearts of the fathers to their children), and the other side is for destroying all false speculations against TheLord Jesus Christ.

> *"For though we walk in the flesh, we do not war according to the flesh, for the weapons of our warfareare not of the flesh, but divinely powerful for thedestruction of fortresses. We are destroying speculations and every lofty thing raised up against*

the knowledge of God, and we are taking every thought captive to the obedience of Christ, and we are ready to punish all disobedience, whenever your obedience is complete" (2 Corinthians 10:3-6).

JAMES and U R2 JOHN will probably pray a prayer like Paul prayed while on his Earthly ministry.

"And take the helmet of salvation, and the swordof the spirit, which is the word of God. With all prayerand petition pray at all times in the Spirit, and withthis in view, be on the alert with all perseverance andpetition for all the saints, and pray on my behalf, thatutterance may be given to me in the opening of my mouth, to make known with boldness the mystery of the gospel, for which I am an ambassador in chains; that in proclaiming it I may speak boldly, as I ought tospeak" (Ephesians 6:17-20).

Will their prayers be answered? Yes!

""Behold, I am going to send you Elijah the prophet before the coming of the great and terrible day of the Lord. "And he will restore the hearts of the fathers to their children, and the hearts of the children to their fathers, lest I come and smite the land with a curse." (Malachi 4:5-6)

The Rider on the White Horse is the Prophet *like* Moses and "like" the Lord Jesus Christ (JAMES).

"These have the power to shut up the sky, in order that rain may not fall during the days of their prophesying; and they have power over the waters to turn them into blood, and to smite the earth with every plague, as often as they desire" (Revelation 11:6).

JAMES will rule over the works of Thy hands. You must understand the purpose of these Two Prophets. They are to usher in World War III (The Second Coming of The Lord) and ending at Armageddon. Thus, people will hate them for their message and for the judgment signs that they will do. They will be the ones instrumental in shutting down the Universe. When they come on the scent the lives of men will be radically changed. The people on the Earth (at that time) would like to go back to Egypt, (when times were good and food was plentiful), but those days will only be in the history books.

The Prophet like Elijah (U R2 JOHN) will shut up the skies for three and one-half years, that will result in drought and starvation throughout the world. Then some people will say, "These Prophets cannot be from God because God promised He would keep us from this hour (Revelation 3:10-11).

These two men are from God, and about one-quarter of the Earth's human population will be destroyed during their ministry.

These Two Revelation Prophets will preach The True Gospel. However, the True Gospel requires repentance (which also requires one to sin no more) and to bring forth fruit in keeping with that repentance.

Bringing forth fruit in keeping with ones repentance means to love your neighbor and take corrective action on the things you weredoing to harm them even before being saved. Plus, you are to stop doing evil things (practices) that many others will continue to do (Revelation 22:10-12). However, you must stop doing what youinternally know to be wrong. You hear people who have spent timein prison say, *"I Paid My Debt to Society."* No, you did not; you received free room and board at the expense of the society, but you did nothing for your victims or their families. A truly repentant personwill bring forth fruit in keeping with that repentance.

""And also the axe is already laid at the root of the trees; every tree therefore that does not bear good fruit is cut down and thrown into the fire. "And the multitudes were questioning him, saying, "Then what shall we do?" And he would answer and say to them, "Let the man who has two tunics share with him who has none; and let him who has food do likewise."

And some tax-gatherers also came to be baptized, and they said to him, "Teacher, what shall we do?" And he said to them, "Collect no more than what you have been ordered to." And some soldiers were questioning him, saying, "And what about us, what shall we do?" And he said to them, "Do not take money from anyone by force, or accuse anyone falsely, and be content with your wages" (Luke 3:9-14 John the Baptist speaking)

Today's preachers mostly leave out bringing forth fruit in keeping with your repentance. So, the big question is, what is fruit? Fruit, are people, but fruit in the Bible includes the love works you do to them to produce people after your kind. Fruit comes from off the branches, but the branches (people) must be attached to the vine (John 15:5). You are to do loving acts to the people on Earth, which will determine what eternal treasures you have stored up in heaven.

""But if your enemy is hungry, feed him, and if he is thirsty, give him a drink; for in so doing you will heap burning coals upon his head." Do not be overcome by evil, but overcome evil with good (Romans 12:20-21).

"Jesus said to them, "My food is to do the will of Him who sent Me, and to accomplish His work. "Do you not say, 'There are yet four months, and then comes the harvest'? Behold, I say to you, lift up your eyes, and look on the fields, that they are white for harvest. "Already he who reaps is receiving wages, and is gathering fruit for life eternal; that he who sows and he who reaps may rejoice together. "For in this case the saying is true, 'One sows, and another reaps.' "I sent you to reap that for which you have not labored; others have

labored, and you have entered into their labor" (John 4:34-38).

"The fruit of the righteous is a tree of life, and he who is wise wins souls" (Proverbs 11:30).

However, in order to produce positive eternal results you must be attached to the True Vine, because if you are not connected to the True Vine you are thrown away as a branch, and dry up; and they gather them, and cast them into the fire, and they are burned (John 15:1-6).

"Do not lay up for yourselves treasures upon earth, where moth and rust destroy, and where thieves break in and steal. "But lay up for yourselves treasures in heaven, where neither moth nor rust destroys, and where thieves do not break in or steal; for where your treasure is, there will your heart be also" (Matthew 6:19-21)

The following verses are what God commanded Ezekiel the Prophet to preach and what He is commanding all of His Witnesses to preach.

Now it came about at the end of seven days that the word of the LORD came to me, saying, "Son of man, I have appointed you a watchman to the house of Israel; whenever you hear a word from My mouth, warn them from Me. "When I say to the wicked, 'You shall surely die'; and you do not warn him or speak out to warn the wicked from his wicked way that he may live, that wicked man shall die in his iniquity, but his blood I will require at your hand. "Yet if you have warned the wicked, and he does not turn from his wickedness or from his wicked way, he shall die in his iniquity; but you have delivered yourself. "Again, when a righteous man turns away from his righteousness and commits iniquity, and I place an obstacle before him, he shall die; since you have not warned him, he shall die in his sin, and his righteous deeds which he has done shall not be remembered; but his blood I will require at your hand. "However, if you have warned the righteous man that the righteous should not sin, and he does not sin, he shall surely live because he took warning; and you have delivered yourself" (Ezekiel 3:16-21)

Jesus used the title *Son of Man* to express His humanity, but in contrast to the Son of Man there is the Antichrist who is "The Son of Destruction – Son of Hell)" (2 Thessalonians 2:3).

Remember, there is a Prophet coming like Moses and like the Lord Jesus Christ (JAMES) who would also be a *son of man* since he is a man, who must warn all people that they should not sin. Those who heed the warning will surely live and deliver themselves along with those who listen to his message.

Wake Up, Listen Up, or Go Down!

"Thus you are to be holy to Me, for I the LORD am holy; and I have set you apart from the peoples to be Mine" (Leviticus 20:26).

People today, even professing Christians, do not want to hear about God's Holiness or even about their own Holiness. They are like the people of old who wanted The Prophets to shut up and stop speaking about the Holiness of God.

"For this is a rebellious people, false sons, sons who refuse to listen to the instruction of the LORD; who say to the seers, "You must not see visions"; and to the prophets, "You must not prophesy to us what is right, speak to us pleasant words, prophesy illusions. "Get out of the way, turn aside from the path, let us hear no more about the Holy One of Israel" (Isaiah 30:9-11).

God, along with the Two Anointed Prophets, want you to repent and to stay on the narrow way. When Jesus was on Earth, He quoted the following verses but ended at verse 2a.

"The Spirit of the LORD GOD is upon me, because the LORD has anointed me to bring good news to the afflicted; he has sent me to bind up the brokenhearted, to proclaim liberty to captives, and freedom to prisoners; to proclaim the favorable year of the LORD, " (Isaiah 61:1-2 and Luke 4:17-21).

Jesus stopped at "To proclaim the Favorable Year of the LORD." Remember both JAMES and U R2 JOHN are the Anointed Ones that bring Good News to the afflicted. However, they will continue preaching where Jesus stopped. These Two Anointed Ones will continue quoting the Isaiah passage about "The Day of Vengeance of our God; to comfort all who mourn."

> *"And the day of vengeance of our God; to comfort all who mourn," (Isaiah 61:2b).*

> *To grant those who mourn in Zion, giving them a garland instead of ashes, the oil of gladness instead of mourning, the mantle of praise instead of a spirit of fainting. So they will be called oaks of righteousness, the planting of the LORD, that He may be glorified.*

> *"Then they will rebuild the ancient ruins, they will raise up the former devastations, and they will repair the ruined cities, the desolations of many generations. And strangers will stand and pasture your flocks, and foreigners will be your farmers and your vinedressers. But you will be called the priests of the Lord; you will be spoken of as ministers of our God. You will eat the wealth of nations, and in their riches you will boast" (Isaiah 61:3-6).*

Yes, the rebuilding of the Temple will take peace from the Earth, but the Great Sword of Elijah, the Word of God (the Sword of the Spirit) will get many saved. Again, the Antichrist cannot build the Temple because he is not yet on the scene, nor will the False Prophet build it. So, before the Two Revelation Prophets are killed, the Temple will be completed. Consequently, the actions of these Two Revelation Prophets will prepare the Temple for the Lord's return.

> *"He who testifies to these things says, "Yes, I am coming quickly." Amen. Come, Lord Jesus. The grace of the Lord Jesus be with all. Amen."* (Revelation 22:20-21).

> *"And there was given me (U R2 JOHN) a measuring rod like a staff; and someone said, "Rise and measure the temple of God, and the altar, and those who worship in it. "And leave out the court which is outside the temple, and do not measure it, for it has been given to the nations; and they will tread underfoot the holy city for forty-two months"*(Revelation 11:1-2).

We see that they *(the Gentile unbelievers)* will *(future tense)* after the Temple is completed tread underfoot the Holy City for forty-two months *(the time of the Antichrist)*. During the forty-two months, The Abomination of Desolation spoken by Daniel, Jesus, and Paul takes place. The last half of the Tribulation is when the Antichrist comes on the scene, and that is the same period of time that the children of Israel will be in the wilderness (Jordan). The Jews fleeingJerusalem will take place at the mid-point of the Tribulation when the Antichrist enters the scene, and the Two Revelation Prophets are killed and resurrected.

> *""But when you see the ABOMINATION OF DESOLATION standing where it should not be (let the reader understand), then let those who are in Judea flee to the mountains. "And let him who is on the housetop not go down, or enter in, to get anything out of his house; and let him who is in the field not turn back to get his cloak. "But woe to those who are with child and to those who nurse babes in those days! "But pray that it may not happen in the winter. "For those days will be a time of tribulation such as has not occurred since the beginning of the creation which God created, until now, and never shall"* (Mark 13:14-19).

The Two Prophets will be acting for the first three and one-half years, and Jerusalem will be their headquarters, and that is where they are killed.

> *"And when they have finished their testimony, the beast that comes up out of the abyss will make war with them, and overcome them and kill them. And their dead bodies will lie in the street of the great city which mystically is called Sodom and Egypt, where also their Lord was crucified"* (Revelation 11:6-9).

The Two Prophets will not stay in Jerusalem throughout their ministry; they will go throughout the cities of Israel, preaching the Good News of the Gospel.

"But whenever they persecute you in this city, fleeto the next; for truly I say to you, you shall not finish going through the cities of Israel, until the Son of mancomes" (Matthew10:23).

Even though the Two Revelation Prophets were preaching for three and one-half years, the vast majority of the Jews are still not saved? Why not? Because the vast majority of Jews do not want to be Jews, they want to be Gentiles. They know the Law is damning and they want to be free of it. For them the best way to be free fromthe Letter of the Law is to make pretend they are Gentiles by calling themselves "secular Jews."

Therefore, when the Two Prophets are killed in Jerusalem the Antichrist takes over and many of those "secular Jews" will followthe Gentile Antichrist rather than putting their faith in their own"favorite Son."

"I do not receive glory from men; but I know you, that you do not have the love of God in yourselves. "Ihave come in My Father's name, and you do not receive Me; if another shall come in his own name, you will receive him. "How can you believe, when youreceive glory from one another, and you do not seek the glory that is from the one and only God?" (John 5:41-44).

Could the building of the Temple on the Temple Mount start World War III? Yes, but it is not yet the time for Armageddon. There will be wars and rumors of wars even during the first three and one- half years of the Tribulation.

"And when He broke the second seal, I heard the second living creature saying, "Come." And another, a red horse, went out; and to him who sat on it, it was granted to take peace from the earth, and that men should slay one another; and a great sword was given to him (Revelations 6:3-4).

Having wars is a sign, but a sign to signify that the Day of the Lord is not yet! God's final judgment, *The Day of the Lord,* comes when people are claiming Peace and Safety; (when the Antichrist is on the scene) and *The Day of the Lord* comes upon them "like a thief in the night."

""And you will be hearing of wars and rumors of wars; see that you are not frightened, for those things must take place, but that is not yet the end. "For nation will rise against nation, and kingdom against kingdom, and in various places there will be famines and earthquakes. "But all these things are merely the beginning of birth pangs. "Then they will deliver you to tribulation, and will kill you, and you will be hated by all nations on account of My name. "And at that time many will fall away and will deliver up one another and hate one another. "And many false prophets will arise, and will mislead many. "And because lawlessness is increased, most people's love will grow cold. "But the one who endures to the end, he shall be saved. "And this gospel of the kingdom shall be preached

in the whole world for a witness to all the nations, and then the end shall come" (Matthew 24:6-14).

So, when should the world's people really panic? When everyone is saying, "Peace and Safety!"

> *"Now as to the times and the epochs, brethren, you have no need of anything to be written to you. For you yourselves know full well that the day of the Lord will come just like a thief in the night. While they are saying, "Peace and safety!" then destruction will come upon them suddenly like birth pangs upon a woman with child; and they shall not escape"* (1 Thessalonians 5:1-3)

So, what these Two Judgment Prophets are saying and doing will bring about the persecution of the Saints, and the continuation of the Apostasy. The people of the world, including many professing Christians, will hate them because they are not Politically Correct. The world's people will also hate all those who are following the Teachings of the Narrow Way. This may not be good news for the people of God, but it is God's plan for saving the most people. This is the plan that brings most people into the Kingdom of God. This plan is the Wisdom and Power of God.

> *"And we know that God causes all things to work together for good to those who love God, to those who are called according to His purpose"* (Romans 8:28).

Remember, Jesus told us in advance what would happen to us:

> ""*But be on your guard; for they will deliver you to the courts, and you will be flogged in the synagogues, and you will stand before governors and kings for My sake, as a testimony to them. "And the gospel must first be preached to all the nations. "And when they arrest you and deliver you up, do not be anxious beforehand about what you are to say, but say whatever is given you in that hour; for it is not you who speak, but it is the Holy Spirit. "And brother will deliver brother to death, and a father his child; and children will rise up against parents and have them put to death. "And you will be hated by all on account of My name, but the one who endures to the end, he shall be saved" (Mark 13:9-13).*

You must endure to the end, and these times will be difficult, because the persecutions were foretold. The Lord told us that in advance.

> ""*Blessed are those who have been persecuted for the sake of righteousness, for theirs is the kingdom of heaven. "Blessed are you when men cast insults at you, and persecute you, and say all kinds of evil against you falsely, on account of Me. "Rejoice, and be glad, for your reward in heaven is great, for so they persecuted the prophets who were before you"* (Matthew 5:10-12).

You have a choice to choose life or death. If you selfishly try tostay alive, you will die physically and spiritually. However, if you lovingly give up your physical life for the love of Christ and the loveof your fellow man, you will have eternal life.

> *""Remember lot's wife. "Whoever seeks to keephis life shall lose it, and whoever loses his life shall preserve it" (Luke 17:32).*

> *""But take heed; behold, I have told you everythingin advance" (Mark 13:23).*

Let's look at the Second Seal of War in Revelation 6 again:

> *"And when he broke the second seal, I heard the second living creature saying, "Come." And another,a red horse, went out; and to him who sat on it, it wasgranted* (by the white horse rider) *to take peace from the earth, and that men should slay one another; anda great sword was given to him"* (Revelation 6:3-4).

Again, if anyone tries to build the Temple in Israel, war is inevitable. However, this is what the Two Prophets will do. Plus, these divisive wars will cause many professing Christians and families to depart from the True Faith and be part of the Great Apostasy spoken of by Daniel, Jesus and Paul.

> *"Behold, I am going to send you Elijah the prophetbefore the coming of the great and terrible day of the Lord. "And he will restore the hearts of the fathers to their children, and the hearts of the*

children to their fathers, lest I come and smite the land with a curse." (Malachi 4:5-6).

Elijah the Prophet (U R2 JOHN) must come *"before"* the Great and Terrible D*ay of the Lord*. No, it is not talking about John the Baptist of Jesus's day, but about one of the Two Prophets in the Book of the Revelation chapter 11. JAMES gives permission to the Red Horse Rider to take peace from the Earth.

"I have come to cast fire upon the earth; and how I wish it were already kindled! "But I have a baptism to undergo, and how distressed I am until it is accomplished! "Do you suppose that I came to grant peace on earth? I tell you, no, but rather division; For from now on five members in one household will be divided, three against two, and two against three. "They will be divided, father against son, and son against father; mother against daughter, and daughter against mother; mother-in-law against daughter-in-law, and daughter-in-law against mother- in-law" (Luke 12:49-53).

Building the Temple in Israel will be divisive, and these conflicts will also bring about the persecution of the Saints. But again, the world's people will hate these Two Prophets and anyone who believes in their Conservative Biblical Teachings.

"And those from the peoples and tribes and tongues and nations will look at their dead bodies

for three and a half days, and will not permit their dead bodies to be laid in a tomb. And those who dwell on the earth will rejoice over them and make merry; and they will send gifts to one another, because these two prophets tormented those who dwell on the earth" (Revelation 11:9-10).

THE THIRD SEAL

And when He broke the third seal, I heard the third living creature saying, "Come" (Permission to Go). *And I looked, and behold, a black horse; and he who sat on it had a pair of scales in his hand. And I heard as it were a voice in the center of the four living creatures saying, "A quart of wheat for a denarius, and three quarts of barley for a denarius; and do not harm the oil and the wine." And when he broke the fourth seal, I heard the voice of the fourth living creature saying, "Come." And I looked, and behold, an ashen horse; and he who sat on it had the name Death; and Hades was following with him. And authority was given to them over a fourth of the earth, to kill with sword and with famine and with pestilence and by the wild beasts of the earth* (Revelations 6:5- 8).

Yes, the wars, famines, pestilence and wild beasts' deaths aredemonically done by Death and followed by Hades, but it is the Two Revelation Prophets who permit them to do so.

Remember that Satan cannot do anything without getting permission from God.

> *These have the power to shut up the sky, in order that rain may not fall during the days of their prophesying; and they have power over the waters to turn them into blood, and to smite the earth with every plague, as often as they desire* (Revelation 11:6)

So, another major problem that the Pretribulationists have is not knowing the difference between the acts of God and the works of the Devil. This problem is major. Why? Because these Two Revelation Prophets are going to bring God's judgments upon the Earth and many professing Christians will depart (fall away from the True Faith) because of what these Two Prophets are saying (preaching) and doing.

Thus, you are to compare Revelation 6 and Revelation 11 as to what these Two Prophets will do to bring about World War III. The Prophet like Elijah (U R2 JOHN) will shut up the sky. Subsequently, the Third Seal is broken, and famine is released on the land. Hunger, starvation and scarcity of food is the judgment of God, but brought about by the answer to prayer of the Elijah like Prophet (U R2 JOHN).

> *"And when He broke the third seal, I heard the third living creature saying, "Come." And I looked, and behold, a black horse; and he who sat on it had a pair of scales in his hand. And I heard as it were a voice in the center of the four living*

creatures saying, "A quart of wheat for a denarius, and three quarts of barley for a denarius; and do not harm the oil and the wine" (Revelations 6:5-6).

Again, famine is the result of these Judgment Prophets, butthe Black Horse of Death is demonic.

"The last enemy that will be abolished is death" (1 Corithians15:26).

Famine conditions will prevail over the whole Earth, and a quick reminder, Elijah caused the famine in Israel during his time, indirectly through prayer. The Prophets in the Book of Revelation willdo the same thing, and it will be a sign of God's judgment. The BlackHorse of Death (by starvation) will follow the famine, and it is a judgment that God permits, and it will be worldwide. All will be affected by this worldwide famine, but the poor will be most affected because of hyperinflation.

Yes, the people of The Way will be affected by the famine, but none of them will perish from starvation, because the Angel of Deathis commanded not to harm the oil or the wine. These two items of oiland wine are symbols of God's Grace (Psalm 23:5). One has to understand that both angels and demons know and recognize those who have the Seal of the Holy Spirit of God and those who do not have it. If you do not have the Sealing by the Spirit of God, then you have the Devil as your father, and he has no problem killing his own.

"But also some of the Jewish exorcists, who went from place to place, attempted to name over those who had the evil spirits the name of the Lord Jesus, saying, "I adjure you by Jesus whom Paul preaches."

And seven sons of one Sceva, a Jewish chief priest, were doing this. And the evil spirit answered and said to them, "I recognize Jesus, and I know about Paul, but who are you?" And the man, in whom was the evil spirit, leaped on them and subdued all of them and overpowered them, so that they fled out of that house naked and wounded" (Acts 19:13-16)

You cannot claim The Faith of the Two Revelation Prophets for your salvation. You must personally believe God and have "Your Faith" in the Word of God, and not have your faith rest on those men. Many people often say, "That's what we believe," meaning that is what our church teaches, but what your church teaches or what those Two Prophets believe and teach is not your faith. Your faith in God's word must be strong. You must believe God and have God's Faith, as recorded in the Scriptures, that gives you righteousness. If you do not have "Your Faith" in God you will be like the sons of Sceva (mentioned above in Acts 19:13-16), where the demons will say something like, "JAMES I recognize and U R2 JOHN I know, but who are you?"

"For what does the scripture say?" And Abraham believed God, and it was reckoned to him as righteousness" (Romans 4:3).

It says that Abraham personally believed God, and as a result of his personally believing God, it was reckoned to his account as righteousness. So, you must be like Abraham, the Believer, and Personally Believe God's Word.

One thing that is of extreme importance is the fact that these Two Revelation Prophets are not coming to start a new religion, church, denomination, sect, or cult. They are coming and presenting the Original Gospel as the Lord Jesus Christ, and His Apostles presented.

"And HE CAME AND PREACHED PEACE TO YOU WHO WERE FAR AWAY, AND PEACE TO THOSE WHO WERE NEAR; *for through Him we bothhave our access in one Spirit to the Father. So then you are no longer strangers and aliens, but you are fellow citizens with the saints, and are of God's household, having been built upon the foundation of the apostles and prophets, Christ Jesus Himself being the corner stone, in whom the whole building, being fitted together is growing into a holy temple in the Lord; in whom you also are being built together into a dwelling of God in the Spirit"* (Ephesians 2:17- 22).

Even though some two thousand years have passed these Two Prophets are part of the True Church that Jesus started.

> *"And Jesus answered and said to him, "Blessed are you, Simon Barjona, because flesh and blood did not reveal this to you, but my Father who is in heaven. "And I also say to you that you are Peter, and upon this rock I will build **My** church; and the gates of Hades shall not overpower it* (Matthew 16:17-18).

The Two Prophets are preaching the True Gospel and not their gospel or their religion. So, when they come, they will present the True Gospel to the world. However, countless in Christendom will not repent. They will stay with their false teachers and their false teachings (remember that the Antichrist is not on the scene during their three and one-half year ministry); however, after the coming of the Two Prophets these Pseudo-Christians will not only be false teachers with their false disciples, they will be Apostates, because then they would have heard the True Gospel, but they will continue to reject it. That is why the Two Revelation Prophets can say:

> *"Children, it is the last hour; and just as you heard that Antichrist is coming, even now many antichrists have arisen; from this we know that it is the last hour. They went out from us, but they were not really of us; for if they had been of us, they would have remained with us; but they went out, in order that it might be shown that they all*

are not of us. But you have an anointing from the
Holy One, and you all know" (1 John 2:18-20).

An Apostate is one who knows The Truth but neglects it and walks away from it.

"How shall we escape if we neglect so great a
salvation? After it was at the first spoken through
the Lord, it was confirmed to us by those who
heard, God also bearing witness with them, both
by signs and wonders and by various miracles and
by gifts of the Holy Spirit according to His own
will" (Hebrews 2:3-4).

So, your faith must be grounded in God's Word. The ThirdSeal continues.

"And when He broke the third seal, I heard
the third living creature saying, "Come." and I
looked, and behold, a black horse; and he who sat
on it hada pair of scales in his hand. And I heard
as it were a voice in the center of the four living
creatures saying, "A quart of wheat for a denarius,
and three quarts of barley for a denarius; and do
not harm the oil and thewine" (Revelation 6:5-6).

A denarius was a day's wage. Accordingly, one would work one whole day for a quart of wheat and another full day for three- quarts of barley. A quart of wheat is probably only enough to make one and three quarter loaves of bread. However, if one combines the sprouted wheat, sprouted barley and a few other sprouted ingredients they can make Ezekiel 4:9 bread, whereby many more could survive. Bread made in this manner can truly be called "The Staff of Life" because it has all the nutrients necessary to sustain physical life and keep you healthy.

The poor will be most affected by the drought, and since businesses will be shutting down and going out of business, onemay not even be able to get a job to get the wheat, barley, and otheringredients. So, be like Joseph and make sure you start storing foodwhile there is a great abundance. Hats off to those who are getting prepared for a catastrophe. They presently do not know what catastrophe they are preparing for, but worldwide starvation will be one of them. However, those who are Preppers must also remember not to be selfish, but to love your neighbors (Romans 12:20 and Luke 3:10-11).

"And do not harm the oil and the wine" (Revelations 6:6). Oil and wine are symbols of Grace (Psalms 23:5), this indicates that none of God's people will die of starvation from the famine. The Scriptures, along with the White Horse Rider, limits the Angel of Death from killing any of The Spirit's Sealed Ones. Yes, times will be tough; and food will be scarce and expensive, but pray earnestly for your daily bread and God will provide.

Those who believe that governments and mother nature are their gods are going to lose faith in those gods. Because most world governments are already bankrupt because of their debt, they continually act foolishly and continually fail to listen to Joseph type conservative Individuals about saving and preparing for a potential downturn in the economy. Our governments have not stored up sufficient amounts of food to feed their people. They have amassed massive debt in good times. So, you can imagine what welfare rolls of debts will be like when companies are shutting down and jobs are being lost. After three and one-half years of drought, these governments will give up trying to feed and take care of their people. They will reach out (Surrender) to the Antichrist who is empowered by Satan to help them out. He will give them his help as long as their citizens take his mark and swear allegiance to him.

> *"And there was given to him to give breath to the image of the beast, that the image of the beast might even speak and cause as many as do not worship the image of the beast to be killed. And he causes all, the small and the great, and the rich and the poor, and the freemen and the slaves, to be given a mark on their right hand, or on their forehead, and he provides that no one should be able to buy or to sell, except the one who has the mark, either the name of the beast or the number of his name"* (Revelation 13:15-17).

> *Elijah was a man with a nature like ours, and he prayed earnestly that it might not rain; and it did not rain on the earth for three years and six months. And he prayed again, and the sky poured rain, and the earth produced its fruit* (James 5:17-18).

Elijah was a man with a nature like ours, thus indicating that Elijah will not come back (No Reincarnation in the Bible --- Hebrews 9:27), but a Christian man Anointed and Filled with the Spirit of God.He will be human with a nature like ours. This man will be like Elijah (for he comes in the Spirit and Power of Elijah, (U R2 JOHN), andhe will do what Malachi said Elijah would do.

> *"My brethren, if any among you strays from the truth, and one turns him back, let him know that he who turns a sinner from the error of his way will save his soul from death, and will cover a multitude ofsins"* (James 5:19).

So, who are the ones doing these things on the Earth? The Two Prophets whose actions bring about God's judgments. Be reminded that the Lord has given them tremendous Power and Authority.

> *(Now the man Moses was very humble, more than any man who was on the face of the earth)* (Numbers 12:3).

Moses called himself the humblest men on Earth. This was not boasting by Moses, but Moses told the people what Power and Authority was given to him by God. Whatever he said and did would come to pass.

In like manner, when Jesus was here on Earth, He was the Humblest Man on the Earth. He was the Word of God who became a Man (the Incarnation) and showed humility by limiting His Divine Powers. He submitted to the Will of His Father and as such — Submission is Humility — "Strength Under Control."

> *"And being found in appearance as a man, He humbled Himself by becoming obedient to the point of death, even death on a cross"* (Philippians 2:8).

Humility is not weakness or meekness. Humility is Strength Under Control.

> *"Have this attitude in yourselves which was also in Christ Jesus, who, although he existed in the form of God, did not regard equality with God a thing to be grasped but emptied Himself, taking the form of a bond-servant, and being made in the likeness of men. And being found in appearance as a man, He humbled Himself by becoming obedient to the point of death, even death on a cross"* (Philippians 2:5-8).

So, when these Two Revelation Prophets come on the scene, one should not judge them by their meek looking appearance (dressed in sackcloth). They will come in the Name of the Lord with the Lord's Absolute Power and Authority. However, also be reminded that these Two Prophets are not Benefactors (Luke 22:24ff); they are Under-Shepherds (Fellow Witnesses) of the Good Shepherd. So, one should *be wise, Wake Up, and Listen Up*. Remember, Wise Men still seek Him!

"And Jesus came up and spoke to them, saying, "All authority has been given to Me in heaven and on earth" (Matthew 28:18).

However, like Moses and Jesus, these Prophets will humble themselves and limit the Power given to them. However, God's people are to pray that these two individuals stay humble and notget carried away with the Unlimited Power that is being given to them by the Lord; because everything they say must come to pass.

So, you do not want them to speak or act out of frustration or anger like Moses did when he struck the rock. You do not want themto strike the Earth unnecessary out of frustration, anger, or even pride.

"These have the power to shut up the sky, so that rain will not fall during the days of their prophesying; and they have power over the waters to turn them into blood, and to strike the earth with every plague, as often as they desire" (Revelation 11:6).

Thus, the Day *of the LORD* is later, after the deaths of the Two Prophets, when God judges the world with His Army of Angels. The Two Prophets not only bring about the circumstances for World War III, but their Message and their actions will result not only in their own deaths but the deaths of some of God's people. Thus, the people of The Way must know that it is God who directs, "Their Individual Lives" as well as the lives of those Two Prophets. None of God's people will be killed without God's permission, (Matthew 10:29-33) and we must remember Shadrach, Meshach, and Abed- nego.

"Nebuchadnezzar responded and said to them, "Is it true, Shadrach, Meshach and Abed-nego, that you do not serve my gods or worship the golden image that I have set up?" (Daniel 3:14).

""Now if you are ready, at the moment you hear the sound of the horn, flute, lyre, trigon, psaltery, and bagpipe, and all kinds of music, to fall down and worship the image that I have made, very well. But if you will not worship, you will immediately be cast into the midst of a furnace of blazing fire; and what god is there who can deliver you out of my hands?" Shadrach, Meshach and Abed-nego answered and said to the king, "O Nebuchadnezzar, we do not need to give you an answer concerning this matter. "If it be so, our God whom we serve is able to deliver us from the furnace of blazing fire; and He will deliver us out of your hand, O king. "But even if He does not, let it be known to you, O king, that we are not going to serve your gods or worship the golden image that you have set up" (Daniel 3:14-18).

THE FORTH SEAL

Again, let us now go back to the Fourth Seal, Death, in Revelation chapter 6:

> *"And when He broke the fourth seal, I heard the voice of the fourth living creature saying, "Come." And I looked, and behold, an ashen horse; and he who sat on it had the name Death; and Hades was following with him. and authority was given to them* (by JAMES and U R2 JOHN) *over a fourth of the earth, to kill with sword and with famine and with pestilence and by the wild beasts of the earth"* (Revelations 6:7-8).

Yes, Death and Hades are demonic beings, but they were given authority to Ride the Ashen Horse, *(by the Rider on the White Horse)* and to kill with sword and famine, pestilence, and by the wild beast of the Earth. Thus, it is Death and Hades that get permission to kill one-quarter of humanity during the ministry of the Two Revelation Prophets. There will be Two Riders on the Asher Horse who will be killing the Devil's people and sending them to Hades. We say the Devil's People because the Ashen Horse Riders are Death and Hades. Hades only follows the death of non-believers; Hades does not follow the physical death of True Believers.

Yes, Death and Hades are names of demonic beings, but it is the Lord Jesus Christ who has the Keys of Death and Hades (Revelation 1:16-19). He, the Lord Jesus Christ, gives the proverbial Keys of Death and Hades to "JAMES and U R2

JOHN." These demonic beings of Death and Hades would like to kill everyone, Believers and non-believers alike, but at this point, they will be limited to killing one-fourth of the world's population which will be close to two billion people.

> *"And when I* (John) *saw Him* (Jesus), *I fell at His feet as a dead man. and He laid His right hand upon me, saying, "Do not be afraid; I am the first and the last, and the living one; and I was dead, and behold, I am alive forevermore, and I have the keys of death and of Hades. "Write therefore the things which you have seen, and the things which are, and the things which shall take place after these things"* (Revelations 1:17-19).

Jesus gave the Symbolic Keys of the Kingdom to an individual called Simon Peter (Matthew 16:16-20), and he was the speaker who introduced the Church to the world at Pentecost. Thus, it will be JAMES, the Rider on the White Horse, who symbolically gets the Keys of Death and Hades, and will introduce the world to the *Time of Jacob's Distress (Trouble)* (Jeremiah 30:7-11).

Again, why will the people of the world hate those Two Prophets? The people of the world will come to understand that it is God and His Two Prophets who are permitting the demonic forces to take the lives of so many.

It is at this point that the 144,000 Jews come into play (Revelation 7:4-8). The 144,000 are not Jehovah Witnesses, nor arethey Jewish Missionaries, nor are they even Believers at this point. They are Divinely Chosen (and Sealed) so that they would not be killed by the Black Horse Rider (Death). This is the quintessence of God's Grace. God is Sealing the 144,000, and they do not even Believe yet, nor do they even know that they have been "Sealed!"

> *"Just as He chose us in Him before the foundationof the world, that we should be holy and blameless before Him. In love He predestined us to adoption as sons through Jesus Christ to Himself, according tothe kind intention of His will, to the praise of the gloryof His grace, which He freely bestowed on us in the Beloved"* (Ephesians 1:4-6).

"The Death Angel recognizes all Sealed True Believers, and he will now recognize the Sealed 144,000 that he does not have permission to kill. These 144,000 will not even know at the time that they are Sealed and Protected. They are Sealed and Protected fromDeath because they are some of the people that God promised would make it into the Millennial Kingdom promised to the Fathers. God is guaranteeing that *"AT LEAST"* 12,000 from each of the Tribes mentioned (Revelation 7:4-8) will get into the Physical Kingdom promised to Abraham, Isaac, and Jacob.

You have probably already heard that the Jews are God's Chosen People; however, it is at this point, when it becomes a reality. God knows these 144,000 will eventually Believe in the future, and by His Grace He Chose them before they even Believed.

"From the standpoint of the gospel they are enemies for your sake, but from the standpoint of God's choice they are beloved for the sake of the fathers; for the gifts and the calling of God are irrevocable. For just as you once were disobedient to God, but now have been shown mercy because of their disobedience, so these also now have been disobedient, in order that because of the mercy shown to you they also may now be shown mercy. for God has shut up all in disobedience that He might show mercy to all" (Romans 11:28-32).

No humans will be able to see God's Sealed Ones, and the only ones to see the Sealed Ones are the Angels (Good and Evil). Even though the Sealing is on their hand or forehead, the Sealing will not be visible with the human eye. However, be warned of the schemes of the Devil. Satan, the False Prophet, and the Antichrist will use those Biblical Sealing Verses to get their people to take the Mark of the Beast. They will get their people to put a visible mark on their right hand or forehead, telling their people it is "The Seal of God," but in actuality, it is "The Devil's Seal of Death."

And he causes all, the small and the great, and the rich and the poor, and the freemen and the slaves, to be given a mark on their right hand, or on their forehead, and he provides that no one should be able to buy or to sell, except the one who has the mark, either the name of the beast or the number of his name" (Revelation 13:16-18).

The Book of the Revelation is telling us how God is going to Fulfill all Righteousness. The Apostasy (Professing believersabandoning the True Faith), and the martyrdom of the people of TheWay will give the Two Prophets confidence that they are preaching the True Gospel. If there was a Great Apostasy, and the Scriptures did not write about it, all of God's Witnesses, including the Two Prophets would wonder if they were preaching the True Gospel. As such, the Judgment Signs that the Prophets Perform are God's Confirmation Signs (God's Declaration) that they are speaking the Truth and Acting on His Behalf.

> *"Children, it is the last hour; and just as you heard that Antichrist is coming, even now many antichrists have arisen; from this we know that it is the last hour. They went out from us, but they were not really of us;for if they had been of us, they would have remained with us; but they went out, in order that it might be shown that they all are not of us. But you have an anointing from the Holy One, and you all know. I have not written to you because you do not know the truth, but because you do know it, and because no lieis of the truth. Who is the liar but the one who deniesthat Jesus is the Christ? This is the antichrist, the onewho denies the Father and the Son. Whoever deniesthe Son does not have the Father; the one who confesses the Son has the Father also. As for you,let that abide in you which you heard from the beginning. If what you heard from the beginning abides in you,*

you also will abide in the Son and in the Father. And this is the promise which He himself made to us: eternal life. These things I have written to you concerning those who are trying to deceive you. And as for you, the anointing which you received from Him abides in you, and you have no need for anyone to teach you; but as His anointing teaches you about all things, and is true and is not a lie, and just as it has taught you, you abide in Him. And now, little children, abide in Him, so that when He appears, we may have confidence and not shrink away from Him in shame at His coming. If you know that He is righteous, you know that everyone also who practices righteousness is born of Him" (1 John 2:18- 29).

The True People of God have this Great Promise:

""And do not fear those who kill the body, but are unable to kill the soul; but rather fear Him who is able to destroy both soul and body in hell. "Are not two sparrows sold for a cent? And yet not one of them will fall to the ground apart from your Father. "But the very hairs of your head are all numbered. "Therefore do not fear; you are of more value than many sparrows. "Everyone therefore who shall confess Me before men, I will also confess him before my Father who is in heaven. "But whoever shall deny Me before men, I will also

deny him before My Father who is in heaven"
(Matthew 10:28-33).

This will be the persecution that Jesus talked about in
John 16:

> *""These things I have spoken to you, that you*
> *may be kept from stumbling. "They will make*
> *you outcasts from the synagogue, but an hour is*
> *coming for everyone who kills you to think that he*
> *is offering service to God. "And these things they*
> *will do, because they have not known the Father,*
> *or Me. "But these things I have spoken to you, that*
> *when their hour comes, you may remember that I*
> *told you of them"* (John 16:1-4).

Those who are killing God's people believe they are
offering service to God, but in actuality they are doing the
deeds of their father the Devil. Presently, like we have been
saying all along that most people do not know the difference
between God and the Devil; however, at this point, you
should know about another scheme of the Devil. His people
will claim that they are Saved and even Born Again Believers,
just like Korah and his people claimed to be part of God's
Holy Congregation. *"And they assembled together against Moses*
and Aaron, and said to them, "You have gone far enough, for all
the congregation are holy, every one of them, and the LORD is
in their midst; so why do you exalt yourselves above the assembly
of the LORD?" (Numbers 16:2-3). You must remember that
you are going out as sheep in the midst of wolves; *"Therefore*
be shrewd as serpents, and innocent as doves" (Matthew 10:16).

257

Those wolves are lying sinners who want you to stop talking to them about the Lord Jesus Christ, His Salvation and His Coming Judgments. So, be warned! They want to suppress the Truth that you are bringing them, because they are the unrighteous.

> *"For nation will rise against nation, and kingdom against kingdom, and in various places there will be famines and earthquakes. "But all these things are merely the beginning of birth pangs. "Then they will deliver you to tribulation, and will kill you, and you will be hated by all nations on account of My name. "And at that time many will fall away and will deliver up one another and hate one another. "And many false prophets will arise, and will mislead many. "And because lawlessness is increased, most people's love will grow cold. "But the one who endures to the end, he shall be saved. "And this gospel of the kingdom shall be preached in the whole world for a witness to all the nations, and then the end shall come"* (Matthew 24:7-14).

These Two Prophets will Preach Repentance from Sin and the True Gospel of the Kingdom. The whole world will hear the True Gospel because of recording devices like television and the internet, and then the end shall come. Matthew 24:10, *"And at that time many will fall away and will deliver up one another and hate one another."* Thus, the ones that fall away will be the ones most instrumental in delivering you up and thus hating one another, because their love of others has grown cold. Family members will be against family members. They will be like the world's people who do not come to the Light, the Lord Jesus Christ, for their deeds are evil.

> *"And this is the judgment, that the light is come into the world, and men loved the darkness rather than the light; for their deeds were evil. "For everyone who does evil hates the light, and does not come to the light, lest his deeds should be exposed. "But he who practices the truth comes to the light, that his deeds may be manifested as having been wrought in God"* (John 3:19-21).

This is the reason for the Great Apostasy that Jesus and Paul also taught.

> *"Let no one in any way deceive you, for it will not come unless the apostasy comes first, and the man of lawlessness is revealed, the son of destruction, who opposes and exalts himself above every so- called god or object of worship, so that he takes his seat in the temple of God, displaying himself as being God. Do you not remember that while I was still with you, I was telling you these things?"* (2 Thessalonians 2:3-5).

These Two Prophets will expose the Antichrist. The Man of Lawlessness will be revealed. So, what must come before the Day of the LORD? The Apostasy will precede the Day of the LORD. The Apostasy occurs because a countless number of people who name the Name of the Lord are not True

Children of God. They are professors but not possessors and are void of the Spirit of God. To understand what is being said, you must understand the simplest of all parables, which is the parable of the sower and the seed.

> *And He said to them, "Do you not understand this parable? And how will you understand all the parables? "The sower sows the word. "And these are the ones who are beside the road where the word is sown; and when they hear, immediately Satan comes and takes away the word which has been sown in them. "And in a similar way these are the ones on whom seed was sown on the rocky places, who, when they hear the word, immediately receive it with joy; and they have no firm root in themselves, but are only temporary; then, when affliction or persecution arises because of the word, immediately they fall away. "And others are the ones on whom seed was sown among the thorns; these are the ones who have heard the word, and the worries of the world, and the deceitfulness of riches, and the desires for other things enter in and choke the word, and it becomes unfruitful. "And those are the ones on whom seed was sown on the good soil; and they hear the word and accept it, and bear fruit, thirty, sixty, and a hundredfold"* (Mark 4:13-20).

This parable contains the simple teaching that one is not saved by faith alone. This parable, along with other Scriptures, tells us about what people did or did not do *after* they believed. If you Believed and Produced Fruit, some thirty, sixty, and a hundredfold you proved yourself to be saved. "You will know them by their fruit" (Matthew 7:20).

However, there are those in the "middle group" that "b*elieved*," but their believing was temporary. They had no firm root in themselves and departed (Apostatized—left the True GospelMessage) because of the persecution that comes with Believing the Word. The other group "the thorn group" of "believers" Apostatized because they were deceived by the love of money and the other worries of the world that made their profession of faith unfruitful.

> *"But those who want to get rich fall into temptation and a snare and many foolish and harmful desires which plunge men into ruin and destruction. For the love of money is a root of all sorts of evil, and some by longing for it have wandered away from the faith, and pierced themselves with many griefs"* (1 Timothy 6:9-10).

The parable of "The Sower and the Seed" tells us about those who depart because of persecution and those who love the world and the things in the world. The works they did after they believed were in vain because they did not produce fruit. Before one believes one is going to be judged as "a sinner," but after one believes they will be judged as "a steward." The steward will be judged on how hespent his/the Lord's time, talents, and treasures after he believed (Luke 12: 41-48)

Even so faith, if it has no works, is dead, being by itself. But someone may well say, "You have faith, and I have works; show me your faith without the works, and I will show you my faith by my works" (James 2:17-18).

So, we see that a faith that stands alone does not stand at all, and the only Faith that is able to stand is the Faith that Produces Fruit. What does a Truly Saved Person do? He "*Produces!*"

"And Peter said, "Lord, are you addressing this parable to us, or to everyone else as well?" And the Lord said, "Who then is the faithful and sensible steward, whom his master will put in charge of his servants, to give them their rations at the proper time? "Blessed is that slave whom his master finds so doing when he comes. "Truly I say to you, that he will put him in charge of all his possessions. "But if that slave says in his heart, 'My Master will be a long time in coming,' and begins to beat the slaves, both men and women, and to eat and drink and get drunk; the master of that slave will come on a day when he does not expect him, and at an hour he does not know, and will cut him in pieces, and assign him a place with the unbelievers. "And that slave who knew his master's will and did not get ready or act in accord with his will, shall receive many lashes, but the one who did not know it, and committed deeds worthy of a flogging, will receive

but few. And from everyone who has been given much shall much be required; and to whom they entrusted much, of him they will ask all the more" (Luke 12:41-48).

Thus, the Apostasy will be great not only because of the Teaching of the Two Prophets, but because many Professing Christians lack commitment. They are lukewarm, double-minded, and fickle. They have adopted a Cultural Christianity but not a Biblical Christianity. Thus, they will depart because they were never really connected to the Vine (who is Christ [John 15:1]). They have adopted a so called, "Easy Believing Gospel," but Biblical Believingis anything but easy.

"For it is time for judgment to begin with the household of God; and if it begins with us first, what will be the outcome for those who do not obey the gospel of God? And if it is with difficulty that therighteous is saved, what will become of the godless man and the sinner? Therefore, let those also who suffer according to the will of God entrust their souls to a faithful Creator in doing what is right" (1 Peter 4:17-19).

Judgment begins with the Household of God. That is the main reason that the Two Prophets are coming to warn the Professing Household of God. Branches must be connected and stay connected (abide) to the Vine if one expects to Produce Fruit.

""I am the true vine, and My Father is the vinedresser. "Every branch in Me that does not bear fruit, He takes away; and every branch that bears fruit, He prunes it, that it may bear more fruit. "You are already clean because of the word which I have spoken to you. "Abide in Me, and I in you. as the branch cannot bear fruit of itself, unless it abides in the vine, so neither can you, unless you abide in Me. "I am the vine, you are the branches; he who abides in Me, and I in him, he bears much fruit; for apart from Me you can do nothing. "If anyone does not abide in Me, he is thrown away as a branch, and dries up; and they gather them, and cast them into the fire, and they are burned. "If you abide in Me, and My words abide in you, ask whatever you wish, and it shall be done for you. "By this is My Father glorified, that you bear much fruit, and so prove to be My disciples" (John 15:1-8).

Remember, the present deceptions and schemes of the Devil are there to deceive you. The Devil, Antichrist, and the False Prophet will increase that deception with signs and wonders that will be so great that even the people of The Way will question what is happening. The Saints are to be reminded that God is permitting the Devil, Antichrist, and False Prophet to do great signs and wonders in order to deceive those who do not believe the Gospel. So, if you do "Believe" the Gospel, do not let yourself be deceived by what you "see" or even by what "you think you see!"

"Do you not remember that while I was still with you, I was telling you these things? And you know what restrains him now, so that in his time he may be revealed. For the mystery of lawlessness is alreadyat work; only he who now restrains will do so until he is taken out of the way. And then that lawless one willbe revealed whom the Lord will slay with the breath of his mouth and bring to an end by the appearanceof His coming; that is, the one whose coming is in accord with the activity of Satan, with all power and signs and false wonders, and with all the deception of wickedness for those who perish, because they didnot receive the love of the truth so as to be saved. And for this reason God will send upon them a deluding influence so that they might believe what is false, in order that they all may be judged who did not believe the truth, but took pleasure in wickedness(2 Thessalonians 2:5-12).

If one does not repent and have the Holy Spirit dwelling in them, they will depart. The unrepentant will be like Peter, who was brave with words but denied the Lord before he received the Holy Spirit. However, he did not deny the Lord after receiving the Spirit of the Lord on the Day of Pentecost.

""For false Christs and false prophets will arise and will show great signs and wonders, so as tomislead, if possible, even the elect. "Behold, I have told you in advance. "If therefore they say to

you, 'Behold, He is in the wilderness,' do not go forth, or, 'Behold, He is in the inner rooms,' do not believe them. "For just as the lightning comes from the east, and flashes even to the west, so shall the coming of the Son of Man be. "Wherever the corpse is, there the vultures will gather (Matthew 24:24-28).

Where the Spiritually Dead People are, that is where the False Prophets (Vultures) will gather. So, you will be able to recognize false teachers by their rotten fruit (the sinning people who continue) to follow them.

"These things I have spoken to you, that you may be kept from stumbling. "They will make you outcasts from the synagogue, but an hour is coming for everyone who kills you to think that he is offering service to God. "And these things they will do, because they have not known the Father, or me. "But these things I have spoken to you, that when their hour comes, you may remember that I told you of them" (John 16:1-4).

Another one of the major flaws of those teaching a Pre-tribulation Rapture is there calling the Saints that die during the Tribulation, *"Tribulation Saints"* (e.g., Revelation 7:14). There is no such thing. There are only Old Testament Saints and New Testament Saints. Pretribulationists only make up this term to fit into their theology of the Church, about not being present during the Tribulation. So, for them, the

Martyred Saints mentioned in Revelation 6:9-11 cannot be New Testament Saints, so they call them *"Tribulation Saints."*

If you call them New Testament Saints than that means the Church is in the Tribulation; which they will not accept, for them the Church is not mentioned after chapter 3 in the Book of Revelation.

However, the Book of the Revelation has twenty-two chapters, and right in the middle is chapter eleven where we read about the Two Prophets/Witnesses.

> *""And I will grant authority to my two witnesses, and they will prophesy for twelve hundred and sixty days, clothed in sackcloth." These are the two olive trees and the two lampstands that stand before the Lord of the earth"* (Revelations11:3-4).

What do these Two Witnesses/Prophets represent:

1. The Prophet, like Moses, represents *the Law.*
2. The Prophet, like Elijah, represents *the Prophets.*
3. The Two Prophets also represent *Israel.* They are the Two Olive Trees—and Olive Tree Branches.
4. The Two Prophets are also the Two Lampstands that represent *the Church(es).* We know the Lampstands are the Church(es) because the Lampstands are interpreted as the Church(es) in Revelation, chapter 1.

> *"As for the mystery of the seven stars which you saw in My right hand, and the seven golden lampstands: the seven stars are the angels of the*

seven churches, and the seven lampstands are the
seven churches (Revelations1:20).

So, we see the Two Prophets represent the Church in Revelation chapter 11. When the Prophecy Teachers say that the Church is not mentioned after chapter 3, they overlook the Church Martyrs under the altar, and the Two Prophets that are mentioned in Revelation 11. Plus, you must take special note of Deuteronomy chapter 18, the Prophet like Moses:

> *"I will raise up a prophet from among **their**
> countrymen like you, and I will put My words
> in his mouth, and he shall speak to them all that
> I command him. 'And it shall come about that
> whoever will not listen to My words which he shall
> speak in My name, I Myself will require it of him."*
> (Dueteronomy18:18-19).

We know that the Prophet like Moses was the Lord Jesus Christ according to Acts chapter 3.

> *""Moses said,* 'THE LORD GOD SHALL RISE UP FOR YOU A PROPHET LIKE ME FROM YOUR BRETHREN: TO HIM YOU SHALL GIVE HEED IN EVERYTHING HE SAYS TO YOU. 'AND IT SHALL BE THAT EVERY SOUL THAT DOES NOT HEED THAT PROPHET SHALL BE UTTERLY DESTROYED FROM AMONG THE PEOPLE." (Acts 3:22-23).

However, the Prophet like Moses in the Book of the Revelation is not from, *your brethren*, the Jews. He is to come from among **"their"** countrymen. Thus, the Prophet like Moses, JAMES, who comes in the Book of the Revelation is an Anointed Gentile Christian; and a Spirit-filled Christian that represents the Church(es). As such, the Church is seen right in the middle of the Book of Revelation. The coming of these Two Prophets is God's declaration that the end is near and that the Jewish people must accept the "Spiritual Kingdom" before they can get into the "Physical Kingdom."

Paul would be happy that his Spiritual Great, Great,... Gentile Grandchildren will be going back to his countrymen --- the Israelites.

> *"I am telling the truth in Christ, I am not lying, my conscience bearing me witness in the Holy Spirit, that I have great sorrow and unceasing grief in my heart. For I could wish that I myself were accursed, separated from Christ for the sake of my brethren, my kinsmen according to the flesh, who are Israelites, to whom belongs the adoption as sons and the glory and the covenants and the giving of the Law and the temple service and the promises, whose are the fathers, and from whom is the Christ according to the flesh, who is over all, God blessed forever. Amen.* (Romans 9:1-5).

Several in the Pretribulation Camp indeed believe that Moses and Elijah are not coming back, but they still have a problem. If the Rapture did happen at the beginning of the Tribulation than whywere not those Two Anointed Christians Witnesses/Prophets taken up in the Rapture? Some falsely teach that, "Two men who previously heard the Gospel (Apostates) would repent and be the Two Witnesses." They have answers for everything but are their answers Biblical? Many of their answers do not agree with the Scriptural Teachings because we know that God would not put a New Believer in such a position, and definitely not an Apostate.

> *"An overseer, then, must be above reproach, the husband of one wife, temperate, prudent, respectable, hospitable, able to teach, not addicted to wine or pugnacious, but gentle, uncontentious, free from the love of money. He must be one who manages his own household well, keeping his children under control with all dignity (but if a man does not know how to manage his own household, how will he take care of the church of God?);* **and not a new convert, lest he become conceited and fall into the condemnation incurred by the devil.** *And he must have a good reputation with those outside the church, so that he may not fall into reproach and the snare of the devil"* (1 Timothy 3:2-7).

If you receive the Holy Spirit, you are a New Testament (New Covenant) Saint. So, what this means is that the Saints are going to go into the Tribulation, and if anyone Believes on The Lord Jesus Christ they will also be put into the Church

(The Body of Christ). Countless numbers will Believe during the Tribulation and become New Testament (New Covenant Saints).

THE FIFTH SEAL

In Revelation chapter 6, it makes this statement about those who were not delivered but were Faithful unto Death:

> *"And white robes were given unto every one of them; and it was said unto them, that they should restyet for a little season, until their fellow servants also and their brethren, that should be killed as they were,**should be fulfilled**"* (Revelations 6:11).

When it talks about being "Fulfilled," it implicitly implies that theMartyrs were killed as part of the plan of God. God does not kill any of His children, but as a result of the preaching and the actions ofthe Two Prophets, there will be many Martyrs. Nonetheless, these Martyrs have to make sure they do not die in vain, but die Witnessing and Testifying for the Lord.

> *""And when they bring you before the synagoguesand the rulers and the authorities, do not become anxious about how or what you should speak in your defense, or what you should say; for the Holy Spirit will teach you in that very hour what you ought to say"* (Luke 12:11-12).

"And He said to His disciples, "For this reason I say to you, do not be anxious for your life, as to what you shall eat; nor for your body, as to what you shall put on. "For life is more than food, and the body thanclothing. "Consider the ravens, for they neither sow nor reap; and they have no storeroom nor barn; and yet God feeds them; how much more valuable youare than the birds!" (Luke 12:22-25).

The Two Prophets in Revelation 11 are God's Prophets and not Satan's Prophets. As such, numerous professing Christians will depart from The Faith because of the fear of persecution, and because they do not have the mind of Christ, and they cannot tell the difference between the actions of God and the scheming actions of the Devil.

However, later on, even after the death of the Two Witnesses, many will know the difference, and they will still follow the Devil. They understand perfectly that it is the Devil who is empowering and controlling the Antichrist.

"And I saw a beast coming up out of the sea, having ten horns and seven heads, and on his horns were ten diadems, and on his heads were blasphemous names. And the beast which I saw was like a leopard, and his feet were like those of a bear, and his mouth like the mouth of a lion. and the dragon gave him his power and his throne and great authority. And I saw one of his heads as if it had been slain, and his fatal wound was healed.

and the whole earth was amazed and followed after the beast; and they worshiped the dragon, because he gave his authority to the beast; and they worshiped the beast, saying, "Who is like the beast, and who is able to wage war with him?" And there was given to him a mouth speaking arrogant words and blasphemies; and authority to act for forty-two months was given to him. And he opened his mouth in blasphemies against God, to blaspheme His name and His tabernacle, that is, those who dwell in heaven" (Revelations 13:1-6).

The fifth seal shows the Martyrs who had been slain because of the Word of God and the Testimony which they had maintained.

"And when He broke the fifth seal, I saw underneath the altar the souls of those who had beenslain because of the word of God, and because of thetestimony which they had maintained; And they criedout with a loud voice, saying, "How long, O Lord, holy and true, wilt thou refrain from judging and avenging our blood on those who dwell on the earth?" And there was given to each of them a white robe; and they were told that they should rest for a little while longer, until the number of their fellow servants and their brethren who were to be killed even as they had been, should be completed also" (Revelations 6:9- 11).

ROBERT "BOB" DOBRANSKI, MDiv

Yes, these are the people of The Way who were killed because of the Word of God, and because of the Testimony which they had maintained. However, at this point; God wants His people to be patient a little while longer, because there are more like them to come, because the harvesting of souls is still in full bloom. So, some of the Saints will be Martyred early in the Tribulation; but most will be killed after the death of the Two Prophets, and many will continue to be killed all the way up to the Rapture of the Church.

> "'And it shall be in the last days,' God says, 'That I will pour forth of My Spirit upon all mankind; and your sons and your daughters shall prophesy, and your young men shall see visions, and your old men shall dream dreams; even upon My bond slaves, both men and women, I will in those days pour forth of My Spirit and they shall prophesy. 'And I will grant wonders in the sky above, and signs on the earth beneath, blood, and fire, and vapor of smoke. 'The sun shall be turned into darkness, and the moon into blood, **before** the great and glorious day of the Lord shall come. 'And it shall be, that everyone who calls on the name of the Lord shall be saved" (Acts 2:17-21).

The correct interpretation of these verses should shock most Charismatics and Pentecostals. These verses are quoted from the Book of Joel and they are obviously "Second Coming" verses. Thus, Tongues (Legitimate Languages) are coming back. No, they are not here today, but this Joel Passage as quoted in Acts chapter 2 was only a Prefulfillment of Joel's passage. All those things mentioned in Acts 2 did not happen at the First Church Pentecost. You must remember that Tongues (Legitimate Languages) are for a sign? Tongues (Languages) are "a Sign of God's Judgment!" Remember God's Judgment at Babel, where God Judged the people by changing their languages, and thus scattering them throughout the world.

> "So then tongues are for a sign, not to those who believe, but to unbelievers; but prophecy is for a sign, not to unbelievers, but to those who believe" (1 Corinthians 14:22).

Jeremiah, the Prophet, preached to Israel about the Judgment of God by a Nation who had a language they could not understand. Jeremiah is saying, "When you hear that Nation people speakingtheir language in your midst (that is foreign to you), understand that,that Nation is judging you at the command of The Lord."

> ""Behold, I am bringing a nation against you from afar, O house of Israel," declares the Lord. "It is an enduring nation, it is an ancient nation, a nation whose language you do not know, nor can you understand what they say" (Jeremiah 5:15).

So, Why did God bring judgment upon the Nation of Israel? The Nation of Israel was in rebellion to God and the false teachers were saying that God was not going to send destruction on Israel because of God's Temple and His presence in His temple. The false teachers were deceptively saying that, "God loved His Temple (His House) so much that He would never let any nation destroy it, and as such the Nation of Israel was protected. Wrong! False Teaching!

> *Thus says the LORD of hosts, the God of Israel, "Amend your ways and your deeds, and I will let you dwell in this place. "Do not trust in deceptive words, saying, 'This is the temple of the LORD, the temple of the LORD, the temple of the LORD'* (Jeremiah 7:3-4).

> *""Yet even in those days," declares the Lord, "I will not make you a complete destruction. "And it shall come about when they say, 'Why has the Lord our God done all these things to us?' Then you shall say to them, 'As you have forsaken Me and served foreign Gods in your land, so you shall serve strangers in a land that is not yours."* (Jeremiah 5:18- 19).

Therefore, unbelieving Israel, God will give you a "Sign!"

When you "hear" foreign languages being spoken in your midst about the mighty deeds of God, you are getting a sign from God about His impending judgments.

> *"So then tongues are for a sign, not to those who believe, but to unbelievers;"* (1 Corinthians 14:22).

When Tongues (Legitimate Languages) were manifested on the First Pentecost the people continued in amazement and great perplexity, saying to one another "What does this mean?" In simple terms Peter tells them they were supposed to listen and obey the Two Prophets God sent to them (John the Baptist and The Lord Jesus Christ), but their leaders did not only not listen and obey, both their secular and religious leaders handed them over to be killed. God is "Faithful" in what He promises and He promised He would "Smite the Land with a Curse" (Malachi 4:6) if they did not listen and obey those two prophets. What does the "sign" of Tongues mean? It means that judgment has come upon the Nation of Israel because she did not listen to the Prophet Jesus that God sent to them. They were "commanded to listen" to Him, and since they did not, He cursed their land and permitted the Romans to come in and destroy their Temple (in 70 AD) and scatter the Nation of Israel throughout the world.

> ""The God of Abraham, Isaac, and Jacob, the God of our fathers, has glorified His Servant Jesus, the one whom you delivered up, and disowned in the presence of Pilate, when he had decided to release Him. "But you disowned the Holy and Righteous One, and asked for a murderer to be granted to you, but put to death the Prince of life, the one whom God raised from the dead, a fact to which we are witnesses (Acts 3:13-15).

So, when the world hears Christ's bondslaves (both men and women) speaking in various languages praising God, the world will also be experiencing multiple signs in the skies and on the Earth. One must understand that all these events will happen before verse 20c of Acts chapter 2; the Great and Glorious D*ay of the LORD.* Cosmic Disturbances are also signs from God, so make sure you "understand" the signs of the times.

> *"AND IT SHALL BE IN THE LAST DAYS, GOD SAYS, THAT I WILL POUR FORTH OF MY SPIRIT UPON ALL MANKIND; AND YOUR SONS AND YOUR DAUGHTERS SHALL PROPHESY, AND YOUR YOUNG MEN SHALL SEE VISIONS, AND YOUR OLD MEN SHALL DREAM DREAMS; EVEN UPON MY BOND SLAVES, BOTH MEN AND WOMEN, I WILL IN THOSE DAYS POUR FORTH OF MY SPIRIT and they shall prophesy."* (Acts 2:17-18).

True Believers already know that different languages, tongues, are a sign of judgment (We know about Babel). Non-believers try to explain why there are so many languages on planet Earth but without success. However, when non-believers want a sign, God will give them the sign of tongues (languages), which is a sign of God's past and future judgments. So, what happened at the tower of Babel?

> *"And the LORD said, "Behold, they are one people, and they all have the same language. and this is what they began to do, and now nothing which they purpose to do will be impossible for them. Come, let Us go down and there confuse their language, that they may not understand one*

another's speech." So the LORD scattered them abroad from there over the face of the whole earth; and they stopped building the city. Therefore its name was called Babel, because there the LORD confused the language of the whole earth; and from there the LORD scattered them abroad over the face of the whole earth." (Genesis11:6-9).

God judged mankind by having them speak in different languages and disbursed them throughout the world. All of God's people know that, but non-believers do not understand because they do not believe the Scriptures. The people of God know why there are over 7,000 languages in the world, but can evolutionist explain how these different languages even got started?

THE SIXTH SEAL

The Terror of the Sixth Seal:

"And I looked when He broke the sixth seal, and there was a great earthquake; and the sun became black as sackcloth made of hair, and the whole moon became like blood; and the stars of the sky fell to theearth, as a fig tree casts its unripe figs when shaken by a great wind. And the sky was split apart like a scroll when it is rolled up; and every mountain and island were moved out of their places. And the kings of the earth and the great men and the commanders and the rich

and the strong and every slave and free man, hid themselves in the caves and among the rocks of the mountains; And they said to the mountains and to the rocks, "Fall on us and hide us from the presence of Him who sits on the throne, and from the wrath of the Lamb; for the great day of their wrath has come; and who is able to stand?" (Revelation 6:12-17) *"And there will be signs in sun and moon and stars, and upon the earth dismay among nations, in perplexity at the roaring of the sea and the waves, men fainting from fear and the expectation of the things which are coming upon the world; for the powers of the heavens will be shaken* (Luke 21:25-26).

When the Universe starts falling apart, then men will finally realize who is doing this to them. Unfortunately, by then, it is too late. They will say to the rocks and the mountains, *"Fall on us and hide us from the presence of Him who sits on the throne, and from the wrath of the Lamb; for the great day of their wrath has come and who is able to stand?"* (Revelations 6:16-17).

All these signs and events have not happen yet, so there is still time to Wake Up, Listen Up, and Repent. *The Day of the LORD* will not come until we see the events and signs that are predicted. As such, there cannot be a Pretribulation Rapture. The Rapture will happen just before *the Day of the LORD* begins. God will take out His Saints and will judge those who are left on the Earth (remember Noah). God will even

Rapture some of those who fled Israel at the mid-point of the Tribulation. However, most Jews that fled to the wilderness will not be True Believers until they say, *"Blessed is He who comes in the Name of the Lord.*

> *""And there will be signs in sun and moon and stars, and upon the earth dismay among nations, in perplexity at the roaring of the sea and the waves, men fainting from fear and the expectation of the things which are coming upon the world; for the powers of the heavens will be shaken. "And then they will see THE SON OF MAN COMING IN A CLOUD with power and great glory. "But when these things begin to take place, straighten up and lift up your heads, because your redemption is drawing near"* (Luke 21:25-28).

> *The Revelation of Jesus Christ, which God gave Him to show to His bond-servants, the things which must shortly take place; and He sent and communicated it by His angel to His bond-servant John, who bore witness to the word of God and to thetestimony of Jesus Christ, even to all that he saw. Blessed is he who reads and those who hear the words of the prophecy, and heed the things which are written in it; for the time is near (Rev. 1:1-3).*

Another major problem with the Pretribulationists is their repulsion against setting dates. They are deceivers and do not want you to know what Paul and others said about date setting.

> *"Now we request you, brethren, with regard to the coming of our Lord Jesus Christ, and our gathering together to Him, That you may not be quickly shaken from your composure or be disturbed either by a spirit or a message or a letter as if from us, to the effect that the day of the LORD has come. Let no one in any way deceive you, for it will not come unless the apostasy comes first, and the man of lawlessness is revealed, the son of destruction, who opposes and exalts himself above every so-called god or object of worship, so that he takes his seat in the temple of God, displaying himself as being God. Do you not remember that while I was still with you, I was telling you these things?"* (2 Thessalonians 2:1-5).

We should let all set dates, and if you know the Scriptures, you can determine if there is any validity to what they teach. The difficulty of spotting false teaches is not in what they say, but in what they don't say. They are shrewd, and cleaver, and they do not want to be caught being false teachers. So, let them talk, so their words will either condemn them or justify them. The Writing Prophets of Scripture tried to figure out the who, what, when, how, and why of the Messiah's coming? So, why shouldn't we inquire and know the times since their writings were written to us and for us?

"As to this salvation, the prophets who prophesied of the grace that would come to you made careful search and inquiry, seeking to know what person or time the Spirit of Christ within them was indicating as He predicted the sufferings of Christ and the glories to follow. It was revealed to them that they were not serving themselves, but you, in these things which now have been announced to you through those who preached the gospel to you by the Holy Spirit sent from heaven-- things into which angels long to look" (1 Peter 1:10-12).

If the Prophets of old and Angels looked for the timing; "Why shouldn't we?" Especially knowing that their writings were for *us*. They wrote for us to understand, and in fact, we should not only look we should know the timing because of the warning signs given to us. This is the way Paul put it.

"But you, brethren, are not in darkness, that the day should overtake you like a thief; for you are all sons of light and sons of day. We are not of night nor of darkness; so then let us not sleep as others do, but let us be alert and sober. For those who sleep do their sleeping at night, and those who get drunk get drunk at night. But since we are of the day, let us be sober, having put on the breastplate of faith and love, and as a helmet, the hope of salvation. For God has not destined us for wrath, but for obtaining salvation through our

Lord Jesus Christ, who died for us, that whether we are awake or asleep, we may live together with him. Therefore encourage one another, and build up one another, just as you also are doing" (1 Thessalonians 5:4-11).

The Pretribulationists have two mantras. The first is this; "The Lord is coming like, "A Thief in the Night."

*"For you yourselves know full well that the day of the LORD will come just like a thief in the night. while **they** are saying, "peace and safety!" then destruction will come upon **them** suddenly like birth pangs upon a woman with child; and **they** shall not escape"* (1 Thessalonians 5:2-3).

The first question you have to ask is, "Who are the **"they"** and who are the **"them"**?" *They* are the non-believers who are asleep, and the Day of the Lord will overtake them just like a thief in the night. All Pretribulationists know the first part of the verse, but do they know what follows? What does the next verse say?"

"But you, brethren, are not in darkness, that the day should overtake you like a thief; for you are all sons of light and sons of day. We are not of night nor of darkness; so then let us not sleep as others do, but let us be alert and sober" (1 Thessalonians 5:4-6).

However, you, *brethren* (the people of The Way, the Saints, the Holy Ones, the Pure in Heart, the Sanctified, the Perfect) are not in darkness, that the day should overtake you like a thief. You are all Sons of Light and Sons of Day. So, let us not sleep as others, do. In contrast to **"them,"** let us be alert and sober; Wake Up, Listen Up, or Go Down!

The second mantra of the Pretribulationists is: "We are not going to be here!" This teaching puts the Saints to sleep, because nothing about End-Time Events will pertain to them, because of their mantra, "We are not going to be here!"

> *"But since we are of the day, let us be sober, having put on the breastplate of faith and love, and as a helmet, the hope of salvation. For God has not destined us for wrath, but for obtaining salvation through our Lord Jesus Christ, who died for us, that whether we are awake or asleep, we may live together with Him. Therefore encourage one another, and build up one another, just as you also are doing" (1 Thessalonians 5:8-11).*

It should be noted that God has not destined us for His wrath.

Being killed as a Disciple of Christ is not God's wrath, but Satan's wrath of blinding men so they would not have Spiritual Understanding.

"Yet we do speak wisdom among those who are mature; a wisdom, however, not of this age, nor of the rulers of this age, who are passing away; but we speak God's wisdom in a mystery, the hidden wisdom, which God predestined before the ages to our glory; the wisdom which none of the rulers of this age has understood; for if they had understood it, they would not have crucified the Lord of glory; but just as it is written, "Things which eye has not seen and ear has not heard, and which have not entered the heart of man, all that God has prepared for those who love Him" (1 Corinthians 2:6-9).

The Scriptures teach plainly that the people of The Way will know when the Rapture and the Day of the LORD will take place. We are not in the darkness, and we will not be caught off guard. The Pharisees in Jesus day were caught off guard because they thought they could see and understand, but Jesus told them they were blind and could not see nor hear.

"Those of the pharisees who were with Him heard these things, and said to Him, "We are not blind too, are we?" Jesus said to them, "If you were blind, you would have no sin; but since you say, 'We see,' your sin remains" (John 9:40-41)

They thought they understood God, but they did not. They thought they had all the answers, and thus, they did not listen to Jesus' words. His teachings did not agree with their

Preconceived Theology. They did not listen to Him. They did not Listen Up, and they Went Down (Your Sin Remains).

> *"'I will raise up a prophet from among their countrymen like you, and I will put my words in his mouth, and he shall speak to them all that I command him. 'And it shall come about that whoever will not listen to my words which he shall speak in my name, I myself will require it of him"* (Deuteronomy 18:18-19).

Just because Jesus did not tell his disciples about the Rapture, and the Day of the Lord, does not mean that Paul did not know and did not tell us. He knew and said this to the Church at Thessalonica.

> *"Now we request you, brethren, with regard to the coming of our Lord Jesus Christ, and our gathering together to Him, That you may not be quickly shaken from your composure or be disturbed either by a spirit or a message or a letter as if from us, to the effect that the day of the LORD has come"* (2 Thessalonians 2:1- 2).

> *"Do you not remember that while I was still with you, I was telling you these things?"* (2 Thessalonians 2:5).

He then proceeds to tell them what events must take place *before* the Day of the *LORD* comes. The Two Prophets are coming before the Terrible Day of *the LORD* to Witness to

Israel and the rest of mankind. So, that some of the world's people will Repent andBelieve on the Lord Jesus Christ. One must have the "Spiritual Kingdom" inside (Christ in you the Hope of Glory [Colossians 1:27]), before one can get into the "Physical Kingdom."

#15 The Second Coming

""And there will be signs in sun and moon and stars, and upon the earth dismay among nations, in perplexity at the roaring of the sea and the waves, men fainting from fear and the expectation of the things which are coming upon the world; for the powers of the heavens will be shaken. "And then they will see THE SON OF MAN COMING IN A CLOUD with power and great glory. "But when these things begin to take place, straighten up and lift up your heads, because your redemption is drawing near" (Luke 21:25-28).

All of the 144,000 who were Sealed missed the Rapture because they did not Believe before the Rapture took place. Then, the Jews who went into the Wilderness (Revelation 12:6) will be escorted back to Jerusalem by the Lord, Himself, who will be preparing Jerusalem and those following Him for Kingdom Living.

"And I saw heaven opened; and behold, a white horse, and he who sat upon it is called Faithful and True; and in righteousness He judges and wages

war. And His eyes are a flame of fire, and upon His head are many diadems; and He has a name written upon Him which no one knows except Himself. And He is clothed with a robe dipped in blood; and His name is called The Word of God. And the armies which are in heaven, clothed in fine linen, white and clean, were following Him on white horses. And from His mouth comes a sharp sword, so that with it He may smite the nations; and He will rule them with a rod of iron; and He treads the wine press of the fierce wrath of God, the Almighty. And on his robe and on His thigh, He has a name written, "KING OF KINGS, AND LORD OF LORDS." (Revelation 19:11-16)

""But when these things begin to take place, straighten up and lift up your heads, because your redemption is drawing near" (Luke 21:28).

This is similar to what Jesus said about Moses lifting the serpent in the wilderness. Looking up is an act of faith, and their confession of faith will be "BLESSED IS HE WHO COMES IN THE NAME OF THE LORD."

""For I say to you, from now on you shall not see me until you say, 'BLESSED IS HE WHO COMES IN THE NAME OF THE LORD" (Matthew. 23:39)

""And as Moses lifted up the serpent in the wilderness, even so must the Son of Man be lifted up; That whoever believes may in Him have eternal life" (John 3:14-15).

The Jews who just got saved by looking up will come with the Lord to Jerusalem. How and why did these Jews end up in Jordan and other countries? They fled when they saw the Two Prophets being killed and the Abomination of Desolation.

""Therefore when you see THE ABOMINATION OF DESOLATION which was spoken of through Daniel the prophet, standing in the holy place (let the reader understand), then let those who are in Judea flee to the mountains; let him who is on the housetop not go down to get the things out that are in his house; and let him who is in the field not turn back to get his cloak. "But woe to those who are with child and to those who nurse babes in those days! "But pray that your flight may not be in the winter, or on a Sabbath; for then there will be a great tribulation, such as has not occurred since the beginning of the world until now, nor ever shall. (Matthew 24:15-21).

Many of these are still non-saved Jews (and many are part of the 144,000), but if they do not heed the Scriptural warning to get out of Judea quickly, they will be killed. Those who do not get out will be considered enemies of God and will be killed by either the Antichrist or the earthquake that follows the resurrection of the Two Prophets.

*"And after the three and a half days the breath of life from God came into them, and they stood on their feet; and great fear fell upon those who were beholding them. And they heard a loud voice from heaven saying to them, "Come up here." And they went up into heaven in the cloud, and their enemies beheld them. In that hour there was a great earthquake, and a tenth of the city fell; and seven thousand people were killed in the earthquake, and the rest were terrified and gave glory to the God of heaven." *(Revelations 11:11-13)

Jesus warned those in Judea to flee to the mountains when they see the ABOMINATION OF DESOLATION. However, they would be wise to pray and do some minor math calculations and flee a little earlier because waiting until the last minute will be very dangerous if not deadly.

""Therefore when you see the ABOMINATION OF DESOLATION which was spoken of through Daniel the prophet, standing in the holy place (let the reader understand), then let those who are in Judea flee to the mountains; let him who is on the housetop not go down to get the things out that are in his house; and let him who is in the field not turn back to get his cloak. "But woe to those who are with child and to those who nurse babes in those days! "But pray that your flight may not be in the winter, or on a Sabbath; for then there will be a great tribulation, such as has not occurred since

the beginning of the world until now, nor ever shall. "And unless those days hadbeen cut short, no life would have been saved; butfor the sake of the elect those days shall be cut short"(Matthew. 24:15-22).

So, the Jews who do not go into the wilderness will be slaughtered. Matthew 24:22, "For *then there will be a great tribulation, such as has not occurred since the beginning of the world until now, or ever shall.*

When the Jewish Defense League says, "Never Again." They better make sure they do not let it happen again and work to get their people to flee Judea in haste like their ancestors fled Egypt. The purpose of this book is to inform all that the Truth will set you Free. God and His people have no secret codes, secret teachings, secret handshakes, or secret societies that have secret writings or mysterious teachings. God is not hiding anything because He is seeking, and he wants you to seek Him. Men are hiding from God because they love their sinful ways, and they do not want their sinful ways to be exposed.

""And this is the judgment, that the light is come into the world, and men loved the darkness rather than the light; for their deeds were evil. "For everyone who does evil hates the light, and does not come to the light, lest his deeds should be exposed. "But he who practices the truth comes to the light, that his deeds may be manifested as having been wrought in God" (John 3:19-21).

"A disciple is not above his teacher, nor a slave above his master. "It is enough for the disciple that he become as his teacher, and the slave as his master. If they have called the head of the house Beelzebub, how much more the members of his household! "Therefore do not fear them, for there is nothing covered that will not be revealed, and hidden that will not be known. "What I tell you in the darkness, speak in the light; and what you hear whispered in your ear, proclaim upon the housetops. "And do not fear those who kill the body, but are unable to kill the soul; but rather fear Him who is able to destroy both soul and body in hell" (Matthew10:24-28).

THE SUMMARY

For if God did not spare angels when they sinned, but cast them into hell and committed them to pits of darkness, reserved for judgment; and did not spare the ancient world, but preserved Noah, a preacher of righteousness, with seven others, when He brought a flood upon the world of the ungodly; (2 Peter 2:4-5).

Jesus said, "His Coming" would be like in the Days of Noah. God always warns before destruction and Noah was a Preacher of Righteousness that saved himself and his family. The Two Prophets in the Book of the Revelation are Preachers of Righteousness that are sent to save the family of God. One in the Spirit and Power of Elijah and John the Baptist (U R2 JOHN) and one in the Spirit and Power of Moses and Jesus (JAMES). If the world's people do not listen to them, then the Lord Jesus Christ will come and smite the land with a curse (*The Day of the Lord*). The reason that the world's people will be caught off guard *like a thief in the night* is simply because they will not heed the warnings of all of God's Witnesses/Prophets.

> ""*I have come in my Father's name, and you donot receive Me; if another shall come in his own name, you will receive him. "How can you believe, when you receive glory from one another, and you donot seek the glory that is from the one and only God?*

> "*Do not think that I will accuse you before the Father; the one who accuses you is Moses, in whom you have set your hope. "For if you believed Moses, you would believe Me; for he wrote of Me. "But if you do not believe his writings, how will you believe My words*" (John 5:43-47).

EPILOGUE

Jesus gives us a great promise about knowing a true teacher. A true teacher does not talk about himself or seek his own glory. That teacher seeks the glory of the One who sent him.

> *"Jesus therefore answered them, and said, "My teaching is not mine, but His who sent Me. "If any man is willing to do His will, he shall know of the teaching, whether it is of God, or whether I speak from Myself. "He who speaks from himself seeks his own glory; but he who is seeking the glory of the one who sent Him, He is true, and there is no unrighteousness in Him"* (John 7:16-18)

"Jesus is giving His Bride a *Special Wedding Invitation*, where He will supply everything needed. He will supply the Food, White Wedding Garments (Matthew 22:11-14), and He will even supply theWedding Gifts. He tells us that everything is ready except the Bride in all Her Glory. Are you ready? Ready or not the Groom is anxiously looking forward to His Wedding Day! Are you anxiously looking toward yours?

"Behold, I stand at the door (of your heart) *and knock; if anyone* (or everyone who) *hears my voice and opens the door* (of his heart), *I will come in to him, and will dine with him* (now and at our wedding), *and he with Me. 'He who overcomes, I will grant to him to sit down with Me on My throne, as I also overcame and sat down with My Father on His throne. 'He who has an ear, let him hear what the Spirit says to the churches"* (Revelation 3:20-22).

"Hallelujah! for the Lord our God, the Almighty, reigns. "Let us rejoice and be glad and give the glory to Him, for the marriage of the Lamb has come and His bride has made herself ready." And it was given to her to clothe herself in fine linen, bright and clean; for the fine linen is the righteous acts of the saints. And he said to me, "Write, 'Blessed are those who are invited to the marriage supper of the Lamb.'" And he said to me, "These are true words of God" (Revelation 19:6-10).

PS: "I have already sent My Engagement Ring!

Have you received Him yet?" (Ephesians 1:13-14).

ABOUT THE AUTHOR

Pastor "Bob" Dobranski was born and raised in Northern Eastern Pennsylvania and graduated from King's College in Wilkes-Barre, PA, with a BS degree in Business Administration. He moved to Southern California in the early '70s and received his MDiv degree from Biola University in La Mirada, CA. He began as an Administrative Pastor but has been a teaching pastor in a small nondenominational church for well over twenty-five years.

Pastor "Bob" wrote another book titled, "John the Baptist's Gospel." It is about man's responsibility regarding salvation. Three groups of people, the multitudes, the tax-gathers and the soldiers all asked John the Baptist the same question, "What shall we do?" John tells all three groups what they "must do" in order to get into the kingdom of God. The Epistles were written to the saints of God in particular cities or geographical areas, whereas this book "John the Baptist's Gospel" was written to the saints of God who are in our Evangelical Churches.